You're On Your Own

(BUT I'M HERE IF YOU NEED ME)

MENTORING YOUR CHILD

DURING THE

COLLEGE YEARS

Marjorie Savage

A FIRESIDE BOOK

Published by Simon & Schuster

New York   London   Toronto   Sydney   Singapore

FIRESIDE
Rockefeller Center
1230 Avenue of the Americas
New York, NY 10020

FIRESIDE and colophon are registered trademarks
of Simon & Schuster, Inc.

For information regarding special discounts for bulk purchases,
please contact Simon & Schuster Special Sales at 1-800-456-6798
or business@simonandschuster.com

Designed by Chris Welch

Manufactured in the United States of America

1   3   5   7   9   10   8   6   4   2

Library of Congress Cataloging-in-Publication Data

Savage, Marjorie.
You're on your own (but I'm here if you need me) : mentoring your child during the
college years / Marjorie Savage.
p.   cm.
"A Fireside book."
Includes bibliographical references and index.
1. Parent and teenager. 2. Parent and adult child. 3. Mentoring. 4. College students—Counseling of. I. Title.
HQ799.15.S29 2003
306.874—dc21   2003042396
ISBN 0-7432-2912-6

THIS BOOK IS DEDICATED TO THE STUDENTS AND PARENTS OF THE
UNIVERSITY OF MINNESOTA, WHO HAVE TAUGHT ME WHAT IS
TRULY IMPORTANT IN LIFE

Acknowledgments

I am grateful every day for the support, goodwill, and good humor of my colleagues at the University of Minnesota and throughout the Twin Cities. These staff, faculty, administrators, and friends share their skills and wisdom freely, to the everlasting benefit of students. There is not enough space on this page to list all of them, so I will do my best to thank them individually.

I would like to express my deepest appreciation to those who have been my partners for years in tackling the daily routines and the occasional crises of parent services—the staff in Student Services Communications: Steve Baker, Deb Parker, Kathy Allen, Barb Carlson, Bill Magdalene, Gayla Marty, and Laura Weber.

The publication process has been a delightful experience thanks to the expertise of my literary agent, Betsy Amster; the initial coaching from my writing instructor, Susan Perry; and the kindness of the editors at Simon & Schuster, Doris Cooper and Lisa Considine.

Finally and most important, continuing gratitude goes to my husband, David Barton, for his love and encouragement, and to our sons, Devor and Noah, who are a constant reminder of all the rewards of parenting.

Contents

You're On Your Own

Your Own

(BUT I'M HERE IF YOU NEED ME)

Introduction

Each day, as I work with parents of college students, I hear variations on a common theme:

> "I hope it's all right that I'm calling. I know my son is supposed to be able to handle these things, but I have a question about his health service bill."
>
> "My daughter is twenty-one, so she's an adult, but can I ask if there's someone who could help her with career advising?"
>
> "I'm sorry to bother you, but I have to talk to someone about a problem my son is having in the residence hall."

Parents apologize when they call to ask for information about their child's college experience. They cannot decide if their involvement is helpful or if they're meddling. They have always heard that when kids start college, parents are supposed to let go. The reason behind every phone call or e-mail, though, is that parents are trying to figure out how to work *appropriately* with their college-aged children and the school they attend.

College is a different experience than it was when today's parents were eighteen, and the stakes are higher. Entrance requirements at competitive colleges are tougher than ever, and the cost of a college education has soared. Most so-called traditional students—those eighteen- to twenty-two-year-olds who attend college full-time—rely at least in part on their parents to fund their education, and families need assurance that their money is well spent and their students are well served.

Just as the college experience is different than it was a generation ago, families are also different. The traditional belief that college students defy their parents' advice is outdated. Today's college students place great faith in their parents' opinions. Neil Howe and William Strauss, authors of *Millennials Rising: The Next Great Generation,* report that most teenagers today identify with their parents' values, and the vast majority trust and feel close to their parents. When students are asked to give examples of real-life leaders, their parents top the list.

I have worked with parents and students at the University of Minnesota since 1993, and during that time, I have seen a significant change in parent-student relations and in family involvement with higher education. Today's parents know more about their student's life than any previous generation. E-mail, cell phones, and Web sites now keep parents up to the minute on what their student is doing and what's happening on campus.

My colleagues at colleges and universities around the country confirm the changes: Ten years ago, parents rarely knew what classes their student was taking; now they know when their child is even *considering* dropping a course. And before the final decision is made, they want information on how a reduced credit load will affect scholarships, health insurance coverage, campus job eligibility, and housing status.

One of the critical developmental steps for eighteen- to twenty-two-year-olds is to learn to make their own choices. Today's students know that thoughtful decision making includes gathering solid information and seeking reliable advice. The youth of this generation realize that their parents have been their best advisers throughout their lives, and they will continue to turn to them while they are in college. Providing guidance from a distance is a new experience for both the student and the family, however, and it requires new parenting and communication skills as well as shared responsibility.

Just as students and parents are working to redefine their relationship for the college years, staff and faculty on campus are also learning how to work with the increased parent involvement they are seeing. Ever since the Vietnam era, when baby boomers insisted that a college's "contract" was with the student and not the student's parents, higher education has addressed students as adults and protected their privacy. Now, as parents, those same baby boomers are swinging the pendulum back, demanding information about their children that they themselves worked to safeguard. College faculty and administrators are surprised, forgetting that today's involved parents are their own alumni from the 1970s, who learned long ago how to challenge and change the status quo.

In this book, parents will learn strategies that will help them work with their child's college or university in support of their student. Illustrated by anecdotes and advice from experienced parents and college staff, the book describes such real-life college and family issues as:

- How to cope with the mood changes of the entire family during the months leading up to move-in day on campus
- Why students complain about the food but still manage to gain fifteen pounds their first year
- Why you shouldn't decorate your child's dorm room
- What to do when your child comes home with a tongue piercing
- What illnesses to watch for among college-aged students and how to make sure your child stays healthy

- When parent intervention is critical
- Ideas for teaching students to take responsibility for their finances

The book is written for parents, but each chapter concludes with a list of Quick Tips for Students, for parents to pass along to their child.

The information in this book comes from my own years of working in student affairs and parent services, and from the experiences of my colleagues at the University of Minnesota and at other colleges and universities throughout the country. The examples cited throughout the book are from our daily contact with parents and students, although names and identities have been changed.

During the college years, parents and their children are developing a new, adult relationship—one based on love and respect—that will last a lifetime. As mothers and fathers move away from the pre-college patterns of closely monitoring and helping direct their child's daily activities, they begin to take on the role of mentor.

Mentoring is a concept that students, parents, and educators can all embrace. With roots in mythology, the word has come to mean serving as a trusted adviser and counselor. It allows respect for a student's individuality and personal responsibility, and it defines a valid and vital role for parents as partners with colleges on behalf of their students.

CHAPTER 1

A Summer of Change

Making the Most of the Months Before College Begins

❧

Every year, as a new group of high school graduates and their parents watch the calendar pages turn toward September, emotions begin to churn. Mothers and fathers who were filled with pride when the college acceptance letters arrived a few months ago will soon find themselves wondering, "How can this kid possibly succeed in college? He can't even get out of bed in the morning by himself."

Students who are convinced that they belong at the college of their dreams are equally convinced a day later that they will never fit in: "I think the school made a mistake when they accepted me. I was probably the last person they picked, and I'm going to be the stupidest person on campus. Besides, I don't have the right clothes. No one will like me. It's just not going to work."

For these students and their parents, the issue is clear: Everything is changing. The excitement and anticipation that peaked in late spring turns to chaos during the "senior summer." Recent graduates are rejecting curfews and failing to show up for family meals, defending their freedom by explaining, "In a couple of months, you won't *ever* know what I'm doing."

Meanwhile, parents are failing in their efforts to maintain

peace in the family. Bickering among brothers or sisters reaches new heights. One parent or the other is locked in conflict with the child. Parents listen to their child's unending complaints about the community and the small-mindedness of the neighbors, and they begin to long for the day when they can finally take this miserable, unhappy kid to college. A minute later, they berate themselves for such thoughts, saying, "I know I'll miss her!"

What's a parent to do? Advice flows in from every direction, but each suggestion seems to conflict with at least one other:

"Give them space." *"No, set clear boundaries."*

"Make sure you talk about the critical issues." *"Don't try to review a lifetime of lessons in one short summer."*

"Tell them you'll miss them." *"Don't lay a guilt trip on them about leaving."*

The whole family has been planning for college for years, but now parents can't keep from wondering if it's what they all really want. When changes are pending, emotional flare-ups are a natural reaction. The challenges are to identify the real issues as they occur and to recognize what each of the various members of the family is feeling.

MAKING DECISIONS: WHOSE RESPONSIBILITY IS IT?

Any eighteen-year-old will react fiercely to parents who ask to see his mail or who want to read the e-mail message that just arrived. Any parent, however, who is facing the prospect of paying for college needs to know that all the paperwork is filled out correctly and on time. So whose job is it to make sure the college mail is opened, the forms are completed, and each of the tasks on the to-do list is checked off? With all the information that arrives each week from various campus offices, who is sorting through the mail and keeping track of deadlines and details? And ultimately, who has the final say in the decisions these mailings require?

From your student's standpoint, these forms will affect the most basic aspects of college life: Will she live in a single room, a double, or a suite? How many meals each week will he eat in the dining center? Should he move into an all-freshmen hall or one with upperclassmen? Students think their parents are encroaching on their personal space when they check the mailings and tell their children how to fill out the forms.

From the parents' perspective, these decisions will affect the family finances, in some cases for years to come. As the parent, maybe you see some pitfalls in selecting an all-freshmen dorm or in choosing a hall with no quiet hours, and you want to help your child avoid the potential problems. Parents feel more urgency about meeting deadlines and more caution about answering the questions completely and thoroughly. They want to make certain everything is done "right," and they want to know how these decisions will affect their child and the family.

When Jeremy opened the application from the college housing office, he didn't think twice about what kind of room he wanted. He wanted a single. Like many college students today, he had always had his own bedroom. After reading the housing application instructions, he quickly filled out the form and gave the papers to his mother so that she could write out a check for the deposit fee. The first thing she noticed, though, was that his single-room selection would cost several hundred dollars more than a double. A triple or a four-person suite would be even more economical.

"Jeremy, you marked down that you want a single room. You didn't even talk to us about this. You don't seem to understand how much it's going to cost for you to go to college. You can't just pile up expenses without consulting us. I think you should consider one of these other choices," his mother said.

Jeremy had plenty of reasons why he would be better off living in a single. He would study better if he were by himself, he said. He needed quiet to concentrate on his homework. He needed his sleep. What if his roommate turned out to be one of those people who wanted to party all the time? What if his roommate wanted to watch television or listen to music until all hours of the night?

In fact, there were other factors at play for both Jeremy and his mother. In addition to the financial impact of the decision, Jeremy's mother was worried that her son might not make friends easily. He had never been particularly outgoing, and his two good friends from high school were enrolling in different colleges. She was afraid that he would be lonely, and it would be much more difficult to meet people if he lived in a single room. At the same time, Jeremy had his own unspoken concern. He had never mentioned it to his parents, but on an overnight band trip the previous year, he was teased unmercifully about his snoring. He didn't want roommates complaining all year that his snoring was keeping them awake.

When they talked through the issues, Jeremy and his mother acknowledged that there were personal and financial complications of this seemingly simple decision. They set the form aside for a few days and agreed to give it some more thought. Jeremy's mother made a call to the nurse at their clinic, who suggested that nasal strips from the drugstore might reduce the snoring. In a moment of enlightenment, Jeremy agreed to a four-person, two-bedroom suite on the grounds that he would have good odds of being matched with at least one other snorer. At any rate, in a quad, he had a one-in-three chance of finding a roommate who was a heavy sleeper. And, as it turned out, Jeremy's roommate was a sound sleeper who went to bed earlier than Jeremy. There were never any complaints about snoring.

Not all paperwork decisions end quite so well, though. Many students, caught up with the closing events of high school or the first lazy days of summer, set the mail aside, figuring they'll get to it later. As the papers pile up, critical responses filter to the bottom of the stack and deadlines are missed.

One afternoon, Melanie was talking with a coworker who mentioned that his daughter was scheduled for orientation the following week. Melanie's son was going to the same college, but he hadn't said anything about orientation. That evening, Melanie asked her son about his orientation schedule, and he said he was sure he had "some brochure or letter about that" in his room. She went with her son to look for the schedule and discovered a small mountain of envelopes and forms from the college.

"What is all this? I didn't even know you were *getting* these things—letters about financial aid, orientation, testing dates. Have you responded to any of this?" she asked.

College mail is addressed to the student. Parents don't always see what arrives, and the only way you will know what needs to be done is if your student tells you. Because federal law recognizes college students as adults, the information goes to the student, no matter who will be paying the bills. From a parent's viewpoint, this might seem absurd; from a developmental view, it makes sense. Students are facing a significant transition as they prepare for college, and they need to begin assuming responsibility.

For Melanie's son, the situation was not as hopeless as she feared—there was a late orientation session he could register for—but he needed to learn some organizational skills. He had an idea of what information had arrived. He just had not yet developed a system for managing records. In a single evening, his mother helped him sort through the pile of mail, using a high-lighter to mark dates and a calendar to note deadlines, and he learned a quick and simple lesson on how to keep his paperwork organized.

With each passing week, your child's anxiety and doubts will intensify. All the forms and letters that are pouring in can seem daunting to a prospective freshman. Every piece of mail is asking for some kind of decision. Some of those decisions are simple, but students might not be certain whether it makes sense to order season football tickets, sign up for fraternity rush, or buy a bus pass that's good for the whole year. Students want to make the choices themselves, but they believe it's critical to make only the *right* choices. Any mistakes feel like clear proof that they're inept.

This is your chance to provide guidance while empowering your student to make responsible choices. Let your child know that you are willing to talk about the choices she's making, but give her authority to make most of the decisions. Let her know if you want a voice on issues that affect finances. If you are worried about health and safety, ask your student to keep you posted on these topics. Tell her she may eventually wish that she had chosen differently, but that will not mean she made a mistake. She is making her decisions based on the information available now.

Checklist for Record Management

Parents and their student can be overwhelmed by all the mailings that come from college during the summer before the freshman year. Which ones *require* responses? What are the deadlines? When are payments due? A few simple tools and organizational skills will make life easier now and will give your child a start in record management for the college years.

Accordion File or File Box, Filing Cabinet, or Fireproof Box

Students will need separate file folders for:

- Housing records
- Finances (tuition and fees information, scholarship and financial aid awards, receipts from orientation, billing for residence hall and dining plan, textbook receipts)
- Health (immunization records, insurance numbers, name and phone number of home clinic or physician, dental information, pharmacy prescriptions, lens prescription)
- Academic information (academic counselor's name and contact information, registration records, lists of graduation requirements, course requirements)
- Computer information (helpline numbers, software support information, e-mail addresses)
- Auto insurance, repair records, and parking information (for commuter students or students who have a car at school)

Highlighter and Calendar or Planner

When a mailing arrives, the student should read it and then determine what action the letter or form is requesting. The student can mark deadlines on the calendar, along with any fees or costs due.

Talk to your child about how detailed the filing system should be; you may agree that information could be separated into more specific categories. Academic information can be further segmented into course planning, career planning, advising records, and transcripts or grade reports. For a first-year student who is unaccustomed to managing records, simpler is better. The more detailed the filing system, the more sections he will have to search when looking for records later—"Did I file that housing bill under 'Housing,' 'Finances,' or 'Contracts'?" As students gain experience, they should be able to handle increasingly complex record keeping.

SECOND THOUGHTS—WHAT IF YOUR CHILD IS JUST NOT READY FOR COLLEGE?

In some cases, those piles of unanswered or unopened college mail are a sign that a student is not ready for the independence of college life. Some students genuinely need another six months, a year, or even longer to reach a level of maturity to handle the responsibilities of independence. Or your student may not know how to tell you he truly doesn't want to go to college.

For these students, as well as for the highly responsible students who want to develop a more thoughtful plan before beginning college, a "gap year" makes sense. Many schools will defer enrollment to allow students to take an extra year between high school and college for work, an internship, or travel. With time to explore interests and draw conclusions about academic and career goals before starting college, students approach their education a year later with more excitement and dedication.

Students begin filling out college applications early in their senior year of high school, and they often make their choices based on the colleges their friends were planning to attend or the school their boyfriend or girlfriend selected. They might choose a college based on a particular career interest. By the next summer, they have a new best friend, their boyfriend is dating someone else, or they have discovered a more compelling career direction. It's too late to apply to another school, but they are rethinking their earlier commitment.

Parents play a critical role in ensuring that students do the right thing at this stage. If it's only a matter of second-guessing or "buyer's remorse," you can assure your child that he does indeed belong at this college. There are good reasons the school sent that acceptance letter. Admissions staff at colleges and universities review applications closely, and they have a good idea of the kind of student who will fit in and succeed at their school.

Unless you know that your student has undergone a significant change in interest, motivation, or ability since the applications were filled out, she will most likely be able to succeed at the school that accepted her.

Most recent high school graduates tread a fine but ever-changing line between maturity and irresponsibility. If you see persistent signs that your child is not preparing for school, you need to find out why rather than do the work yourself. It will be a disservice to you and your child if you step in, take care of the paperwork and packing, and send him off when he is not ready or doesn't want to go. As hard as it may be to keep an eighteen- or nineteen-year-old home another year, it can be a better option than sending him off to certain failure.

"LAST TIME" SYNDROME

As you sit at the picnic table in the backyard in mid-July, a wave of nostalgia washes over you. "She'll be leaving soon! This could be the last picnic we have together," you think. A similar nostalgic feeling overcomes you on the way to church, at the mall, watching TV, or curling up with a book on a rainy Sunday afternoon.

Some parents try so hard to savor each moment that they end up in a constant state of depression. Others react with frustration at every complaint and miss the good times. This last summer before college is a series of emotional peaks and valleys. Your feelings might be different for your first child, a middle child, or the youngest, but no matter what, there will be trying times.

Where I work, new student orientation begins in June and continues into July. During the first week of orientation, parents have just finished cleaning up after the high school graduation party, and they have no problem with the notion that their student will be moving away from home in a few months—September is still too far away to take it all seriously. By early July, though, I start to see parents in tears when they realize that their child will soon be leaving for college: "I promised myself I wasn't going to cry. I'm just not ready for him to grow up!"

And it's not only the mothers who are affected by the transition. A father will gulp back the lump in his throat when he watches his daughter walk away with her orientation group.

A family arrived for orientation one morning in July. The daughter registered under the watchful gaze of her mother and father; then they all crossed the room to the check-in table for parents. When the father couldn't find name badges for himself or his wife, he began berating the student volunteer who was staffing the information desk. "We signed up for this program a month ago! How can you say our names aren't on the list? This is ridiculous! I want to talk to your supervisor. Now!"

The intensity of his reaction was a surprise to the staff as well as to his wife and daughter. His daughter finally remembered that she had rescheduled her orientation date, and she had forgotten to change the registration for her parents. Their names were simply on a list for the next day's program. After the problem was solved and the family moved into the auditorium, the man's wife returned to the registration table to explain that this was their youngest child and their only daughter: "Our boys both went to a college just a few miles from home, so it didn't feel that far away. And my husband has always been very protective of our daughter. I think this is really hard for him."

It is common for parents to become critical about the college or university in the last few weeks before school begins. Patience wears thin as the rosy glow of the *image* of sending their student to college collides with the stark reality of both the costs they will be facing and their student's approaching independence. Anything about the school that seems less than perfect is cause for alarm. A mother wonders how smart the residence hall director is if he doesn't know how much space there will be under her son's bed. "I have to get him a storage box that will fit under his bed. And you don't even know how high the beds are? Have you ever even *been* in the dorm rooms?"

The mother who is accusing hall directors of neglecting their duties before her son even moves into the hall is actually worried that she will not be around to make sure her boy is safe. Fathers are asking college administrators if they have run background checks on campus security monitors, when the real fear is that their daughter will be walking alone on campus at night. They advise the college to "close down those irresponsible fraternities," when the concern actually is that their son got drunk at a friend's cabin over the weekend.

The emotions you feel as school approaches are legitimate and real. You deserve rational explanations and full answers to your questions. But try to ask yourself, when you begin to fume, if your frustration is with the school, your student, or the larger situation—your family is changing, and you are going to have to trust someone else with your very precious child.

"BUT I HAVE *PLANS!*"

As the end of summer approaches, parents wonder if they have lost all control. They try to schedule a family weekend before their son leaves for college, but he has something else lined up for each date they suggest. They would like to take him shopping, but he is booked every evening for the next week and a half. They expect him home for supper, but he doesn't show up. He is always "hanging out with friends."

The last few weeks before college, students are not focusing on packing, cleaning their room, or spending time with family. They are spending all their time with their high school classmates, making every effort to cement the friendships they are leaving.

At this moment in your child's life, he has much more in common with his friends than he does with you.

The senior summer holds magical moments for soon-to-be college students. During the day, prospective freshmen are working their separate jobs, being treated like adults. Every evening, and stretching long into the night on weekends, they are out with their friends, picturing all the possibilities the future holds. And they believe in their dreams. She will, indeed, be an international law attorney working in Paris, and ten years from now, she will fly to New York for the opening of her best friend's Broadway play. This is, for many students, the best social period of their lives so far, and while it's easy to imagine a great future in distant and exotic lands, it is impossible to think about leaving these friends from home in just a few weeks.

The significant developmental factor is that these young men and women are now looking outward, toward their peers and away from their family, as part of the maturing process. They have learned how to relate to people who are somewhat different from themselves (although so far, not *too* different), how to hold a conversation, how to manage their own behaviors. These are all skills that young adults—and college students—need in order to succeed. Right now, even though life is easy and comfortable because the faces are familiar, it feels new and exciting because the boundaries are expanding.

Your expectations that your child will take time away from friends in order to have dinner with you, to go to the mall with the family, or to pack a few boxes seem to your child like a tremendous affront. Home and family don't have that tinge of thrill that comes with being out in the world. After all, you've always been there for your child, and she fully expects that you always will be.

During these last few weeks at home, your child isn't quite sure what to think about you. When you tell your son what to do, he is resentful that you still treat him like a child; if you leave him alone to make his own decisions, he feels as though you're abandoning him. If you remind your daughter about packing, you're nagging; if you don't offer to look for boxes, you obviously don't care about her or respect her educational plans.

Your child is midway between childhood and adulthood, and every step forward is made with the assumption that things are still solid at home but with the fear that they are not. Thinking about leaving home is both exciting and frightening, but young adults don't dare express their concerns about the upcoming changes. Instead they just become angry or aloof.

The turmoil will be visited upon both parents and siblings. The biggest problems seem to crop up between the student and whichever parent he or she most closely resembles. It's hard to imagine major confrontations as a compliment, but if you and your daughter are arguing constantly, and you're wondering how you could have become such a dreadful parent, this is probably a sign that she is much like you. And that thought annoys her endlessly.

Younger brothers or sisters begin to see great possibilities for themselves as they watch the freshman prepare for college. They're imagining their own transition to college someday, which seems pretty exciting from the vantage point of a fourteen- or sixteen-year-old. At the same time, they're seeing some personal potential in their sibling's departure. "Do I get to move into her bedroom now?" "If she gets a new computer, I should get one too." "He's going to college, so I get his car!"

Just when your soon-to-be college student feels that all the lights should be shining brightly on him, his little sister is demanding all the attention, it feels as if Dad wants him around only to mow the lawn, and Mom is enthusiastically buying him laundry detergent, deodorant, and new underwear. To the departing child, this all adds to a slowly festering suspicion: "Everyone is a little too happy that I'm leaving."

LAST-MINUTE ADVICE

All across the country, as long July days fade into sweltering August nights, parents of college-bound freshmen lie awake perspiring with dread as much as with heat: "Can he balance a checkbook?" "What will she do if she gets sick?" "I don't think she understands how much trouble she can get into for underage drinking."

You have only a few more weeks to pass along all the advice your child needs to know. How will you cover it all, and what happens if you forget to mention something important?

High school graduates, however, rarely listen patiently as their parents deliver warnings about campus safety or lectures on how the family's health insurance works.

There are things your student needs to know for the purely practical demands of coping with life in a new situation. There are things your student's college *wants* you to discuss with your child. There are even a few things your child would appreciate hearing from you. The trick is to figure out when you're offering useful information as opposed to unwanted advice or an index of admonishments. All students should know how to:

- *Do their own laundry.* This skill includes, at minimum, sorting delicates for hand washing; removing tissues, dollar bills, and other paper from pockets; separating reds, purples, and maroons from light colors; measuring laundry detergent; knowing what *not* to wash (most notably sports jackets, ties, and anything that is labeled "Dry Clean Only"); and keeping wool sweaters away from hot water and dryers. If possible, continue the laundry lesson with additional suggestions for separating jeans and dark clothes from light colors; using fabric softener; loosely loading clothes into washer and dryer, rather than stuffing a whole week's worth of laundry into a single load; and removing clothes from the dryer soon after the machine stops. (Shopping tips: Most students do very well with a wardrobe of T-shirts, sweatshirts, jeans, and easy-care pants and shorts.)

- *Balance a checkbook and manage a debit card or credit card.* Ideally, your child should have been learning about checkbooks, debit cards, or credit cards during the last years of high school. By the time college classes begin in the fall, he or she should understand the importance of recording debit and check deposits and withdrawals and the mechanics of reconciling a bank statement. Please talk to your student about the potential hazards of credit card debt and explain about late-payment penalties, interest charges, and annual fees. More information about finances can be found in chapter 5.

- *Iron a shirt, replace a button, repair a ripped seam.* Be pitiless about insisting your student take care of his or her wardrobe during the summer. You will probably never get a thank you, but at least your child will have the ability to maintain a decent appearance.

- *Prepare or obtain basic food.* A missed meal means students must occasionally find food to get through the night. Residence hall staff are often dismayed at their students' inability to read the instructions on popcorn packages—or to clean up the orange residue in the microwave when the bag burns. Make sure your child has, at least once in his or her life, called in an order for pizza and paid the driver the appropriate sum plus a reasonable tip. Some first-year students become quite indignant when they find out they are being charged sales tax and maybe a delivery fee.

- *Trust their instincts when they feel uneasy or unsafe.* Most parents remember to tell their daughter to avoid walking across campus alone at night. Young men need the same message. Also talk to your student about date rape and acquaintance rape. Students enter into new friendships with great trust and confidence, and they often ignore or downplay suggestive and threatening behaviors. More information on this topic is presented in chapter 6.
- *Make responsible decisions regarding alcohol and drugs.* The opportunity for partying will be far greater at college than ever before. Remind your student of your expectations, and encourage him or her to be careful. Alcohol and drugs are discussed more fully in chapter 6.
- *How to change a tire, where to go for an oil change, how to operate a car wash (if they will have a car at school or if they are commuting to school).* If your student spends more time worrying about or reacting to any of these issues than on studying, he or she should probably not have a car at school. Students should also know what to do if there is an accident and how to respond if they are stopped by the police.

Throughout that last summer at home, you will think of things you want your child to know before she leaves. Your tendency might be to call her into the kitchen as a topic pops into your mind while you're fixing dinner or reading the newspaper. Your daughter, however, won't be in any mood to pull herself away from the computer to submit to what sounds to her like another lecture. Some parents have suggested they have more success when they set an appointment with their student and explain why the subject is important:

> "When I do the taxes next winter, I'm going to need some information from you about some of your college expenses. I'd

like to spend an hour or so with you on Saturday to figure out how you can track those expenses in your checkbook this year. Can we plan to work on it right after lunch on Saturday, say at around one o'clock?"

"I notice you're getting a lot of credit card applications in the mail. I get those all the time, too. I'd like to talk to you about the fine print on some of those applications so that you can see what the actual costs are."

PARENTS WHO DO TOO MUCH

It is exciting for you, as a parent, to imagine this new life your child is about to begin at college. Perhaps you envision your daughter living in a residence hall, and you picture her friends flocking into her room because it is so warm and inviting. You want her to have nice things, and soon you find yourself shopping for a bright comforter and small appliances in coordinated colors. The next thing you know, you're on the phone calling the housing staff to find out if the doors in her room are wooden or magnetic so that you can buy the right kind of message board.

As much fun as it can be to think about your child's life at college, this is not the time to take charge of every detail. Instead of picking out matching sheets, towels, and lampshades, encourage your student to make a call or send an e-mail to her new roommate to talk about what they each will bring. Discussions between roommates about how to decorate the room can be among the most useful steps in learning about one another.

Every year, in every residence hall, there is a student who arrives a few hours after his roommate and finds the walls already plastered with posters, a futon and inflatable chair taking up two-thirds of the floor space, a CD player loaded with six disks set to play at random for the next three hours, and a bicycle suspended from a hook on the ceiling. The only unadorned space in the room is a single unmade top bunk and the surface of one dresser. The latecomer gets the instant message that he is an intruder in his own room. If he doesn't like the bike hanging in front of his closet or if his bookshelf isn't going to fit, he won't even be able to talk about it until the music stops.

By planning and setting up the room together, new roommates pick up useful clues about one another's personality, values, background, and financial resources. A shopping trip is often the students' first shared outing. Your role, as a parent, is to encourage your student to use these decisions as a way to meet roommates, share ideas, and find ways to compromise.

Although you cannot get your child ready for college, you can help by breaking down the task. Instead of telling your daughter to start packing, suggest that she find a carton and pack linens (or toiletries or computer supplies). Focusing on a single category at a time makes the job more manageable. She can also make her own packing list by thinking through her daily routine. What will she need as she showers and gets ready for class in the morning? What will she want to have on her desk when she's studying? On a cold, rainy day, what extra clothes will she need?

Students do not have to bring everything they own. Hall directors advise, "If your possessions won't fit into a minivan, they probably won't fit into a residence hall room." Some parents have found that it's both affordable and efficient to box and ship their child's belongings rather than haul them across the country: "He was willing to limit himself to four cartons of clothes, books, and supplies and ship them ahead, as long as we agreed to let him bring his computer in the car."

Most students do not want you to help with the packing, but they will not complain if you offer to put together some specific items—a get-well kit in case they come down with a cold, a batch of cookies or study rations to get them through the first week, or a tool kit for basic repairs and computer setup. You can also offer to take on a peripheral task, such as washing and folding all your child's laundry this one last time (while emphasizing that you will *not* accept packages of dirty laundry every week while your student is in college).

COMMUTER CONCERNS

As high school friends are talking about leaving for college, commuter students begin to question their decision to stay home. Natalie had decided to enroll in a community college as a way to save money. Unfortunately, the two-year college in her town was just three miles from home and within sight of her old high school. By the beginning of August, she was disappointed that she had passed up any other opportunities she might have had, and she was envious of all her friends who were getting ready to leave. She couldn't work up any enthusiasm about college. As they thought about the first day of classes, only two things entered her mind: "Where am I supposed to park?" and "Who am I going to hang out with?"

She also had a nagging suspicion that college should somehow feel more important to her than it did. Her friends' parents were all taking a couple days off work to go with their children to new-student orientation; her own parents merely left a note before they went to work on the morning of Nat's orientation— "Hope your day goes well! See you tonight." Her friends were comparing their experiences of opening bank accounts in their college town and talking about first phone calls with new roommates. For Natalie, nothing about college seemed different or exciting. When she came home from orientation, she complained to her mother, "The only time they offer Spanish is in the evening, and it's taught by Mrs. Jenkins from my high school. It's going to be just like last year."

For students who will be commuting to a university where

most freshmen live in the dorms, the feelings of resentment are even stronger. They attend orientation, and everyone is asking "So, where are you from? What hall will you be living in?" The commuter is convinced that it's far more interesting to be the girl from Florida or the guy from Seattle than the kid from six miles away. Admitting that he's living at home—with his parents—is essentially saying, "I'm boring to the bone."

All these emotions are expressed to parents not as frustrations, but as disinterest. Commuter students often act as though college is not particularly important, and it can be hard for parents to work up enthusiasm about the college experience when they see so little excitement from their child.

The little things you do before school starts can make a great difference, though. If the school has a parent orientation, your attendance will show your child that you value his college experience and his choice of schools. By scheduling a checkup on the car, your child will see that you think his commute is important. By talking about changes in family chores and granting more flexibility for household responsibilities, you will let your student know that you understand and respect the fact that college is more demanding than high school, and that you are proud of your child's academic efforts.

QUICK TIPS FOR STUDENTS

- Review college mailings as they arrive, figure out what response is needed, and reply as soon as you can. And start thinking about what you will want to take with you to school.
- Tell your parents about decisions that have a significant financial impact. If you must ask your parents to take on any unexpected expenses, give them your reasons for needing or wanting to incur the extra cost. If they can't add any more to their budget, figure out if you can fund the expense yourself.

- Be certain you can do your laundry, iron a shirt, and replace a missing button. If you will be taking a car to campus, know how to change a tire, when to schedule an oil change, and what to do if you are stopped by the police. Assume these responsibilities during the summer, and you will have less to learn when you get to college.
- Don't save packing for the last minute. Break the job into smaller tasks, so it won't seem so overwhelming.
- Be prepared to ask for help, and you'll get it. Every college has faculty and staff who can talk to you about what classes to take, how to get along with roommates—people to talk to if you're unhappy.

CHAPTER 2

Reality Bites

Establishing New Patterns

T he day your student leaves home for college is a pivotal point in the change you are making from your role as primary care-taker and supervisor for your child to the role of proud mentor and supporter. The process is exciting, but it includes a degree of pain.

When we took our oldest son to college, I was confident that we all were ready for this step. I was certain I would be more pleased to see him begin this next stage of his life than sad about his departure.

We turned the journey into a family event. We packed our two vehicles, both loaded to capacity, for a three-day road trip from Minnesota to Houston, Texas. With my husband and me in one car and our two sons in the other, we headed south. We carefully planned meeting points for meals and hotel stops along the route so that we could change drivers and make sure the cars were both running well.

When we arrived in Houston and found the residence hall, we stood by as our son checked in at the front desk. The student worker on duty welcomed him and gave him his room key, a map of the building, and a two-page handout on bright yellow paper, covered with bullet points and bold type. "These are your hurricane instructions," I heard him say to my son. "There's a hurricane just off the coast, and it's supposed to come ashore sometime during the night. If it does, we'll be knocking on doors to get everyone up and moved into the hallways."

I had been so confident that we had prepared our son for everything he would need to know for college, but hurricane survival tips had never entered my mind. I stepped up to the desk and said, "We've been reading all the information the university was sending us, and there was never any mention of hurricanes. How were we supposed to know about hurricanes? We're from Minnesota."

"That's OK," the student said. "We know what to do. We'll take care of him."

This tall, lanky, straggly-haired kid—who obviously would be blown away by a strong gust of wind—was supposed to protect my son from a hurricane?

As hard as it was to accept, I had to admit that things would happen during the next four years that I had never predicted, and that I could not prepare my son for every contingency. I needed to trust his judgment, and I needed to have confidence in the staff at this university. As they reminded us at parent orientation, fully trained, professional, and caring counselors, advisers, and student services personnel were on duty to deal with not only the typical problems that students experience, but also any emergency situations that may arise.

HOW WILL ALL THIS STUFF FIT INTO A DORM ROOM?

Until now, college was the future—something to look forward to and prepare for. Once students start packing the car, though, the dream becomes reality. A father describes his son, loading boxes into the van, suddenly turning to his parents and saying, "I'm not ready. Sure, I've got everything packed, but it's me—*I'm* not ready."

Talkative children become silent as they get closer to their college town. Quiet students chatter nervously. Arguments crop up over minor points. One student remembers the trip from his home in Virginia to college in Arizona as a cross-country argument with his younger sister, who insisted on sitting in the front seat the entire way. A mother recalls driving the width of Pennsylvania in silence following an argument with her daughter. One year, when I was helping move students into a residence hall on move-in day, I watched as a car pulled up to the curb and the freshman in the front seat nervously scanned the scene of people hauling boxes, laundry baskets, and sports equipment across the lawn. He opened his door, walked to the back of the car, and threw up.

Students aren't the only ones who are frightened and emotional. Parents are on edge, and anything that fails to go as planned serves as evidence that the student should return home immediately. The father who finds a line of people waiting for the elevators will be convinced that the dorm is poorly designed—an architectural nightmare. A mother who sees a box elder bug on her daughter's windowsill will capture it in a plastic bag to prove to the hall staff that the room is not habitable. As student services professionals explain, anger and sadness stem from the same underlying feeling: "I want my child back."

Although parents can't prevent their student or themselves from being nervous, they can help make the move-in process less traumatic. The last thing your child wants on move-in day is for the family to make a scene. While you and your husband may think you're being supportive by wearing T-shirts in the school's yellow-and-black colors, your student would much prefer that on this, of all days, you fade into the background in nondescript khaki. Your intentions may be good as you seek out the hall director to have her meet your son and hear about his dust allergies, but your son would rather slip anonymously into his room.

Mothers and fathers can take heart, however, that their student is already beginning to see them as more desirable parents than some of the alternatives. Although your daughter may seem shockingly embarrassed by you on move-in day, she will also be noticing that her parents are not nearly as bad as the family in the room down the hall.

So what is the recommended plan for move-in day? Do you unload your student's belongings at the curb and drive away? Do you plan to spend the weekend making certain that your child finds his classes and meets at least one new friend?

The first recommendation is to take the most direct route to campus. Many parents, especially fathers, like to think that the one thing they can do for their child on this last "family weekend" is to plan a nice, leisurely trip to college with a stop along the way for an hour-long hike at a park, a picnic lunch, and maybe a side trip to go to a ball game or to visit the relatives who live nearby. Your student, however, is not in the mood for a vacation. She is worried, excited, and intent upon getting to school. Your efforts to give her a memorable farewell trip will be unappreciated. Save the scenic route for the trip home or for next year.

If you must do something to keep your mind off your child's departure, put your energy into fussing over the car rather than trip planning. Clean out the car; vacuum the trunk; get the oil checked; replace the windshield wipers; put air in the tires. Any maintenance that prevents a breakdown en route to college is a good investment in family harmony. The freshman stuck on the side of the road with her family, in a stuffy car filled with every one of her earthly possessions, waiting for a tow truck, is a sure candidate for emotional meltdown.

Soon enough, your daughter, lugging a cardboard carton topped with her pillow, will walk into the room that will be the center of her life for the next eight and a half months. The focal point, the bed, will look stark and uninviting. As she drops the box on the floor and tosses her pillow onto the gray-striped, plastic-covered mattress, you will see the mix of excitement and dread on her face.

"I thought it would be bigger," she might say as she looks around. "Two of us are supposed to fit in here? Is that really the only closet?"

By my count, the average college student today brings at least fourteen electrical appliances to school. Multiply that by the number of roommates, and the challenge becomes clear: living in a residence hall is a constant exercise in adaptation, and unpacking is the student's first step in learning to "make do." For parents, move-in day is a pop quiz in the course of relinquishing responsibility for your child. Your son or daughter will not approach the move-in and unpacking as you would. This task, however, belongs to your child, and throughout the process, you must help only if you're asked.

Your student will appreciate assistance carrying things up to the room, and most students accept their mother's offer to make the bed. Depending on the student's own technical ability, the majority are willing to let a parent or sibling help set up the computer. Beyond that, though, students usually prefer to do their own unpacking in their own time. Tempers become short when a parent suggests which drawer the underwear belongs in or where the family photo should be placed.

And this is not the time to remind your daughter that you told her she would never be able to fit everything she brought into her dorm room.

Younger brothers and sisters are intrigued by this new place, envious of their older sibling, and often at least a little disconcerted by the prospect of leaving their big brother or sister here. A burst of jealousy is common as the younger child demands attention. Steph recalls her twelve-year-old brother insisting that the first thing she should unpack was her new microwave so that he could make popcorn. To stop his whining, she dug the microwave out of the pile of boxes and let him plug it in. As she turned to arrange her closet, her brother managed to scorch the popcorn, sending out waves of smoke and an offensive odor that lingered not only in her room but also throughout the entire hallway, for the rest of the afternoon.

When your student shows signs of irritation, it's usually best for the rest of the family to take a break. A visit to the college's art gallery, a campus tour, or a two-hour trip to a nearby tourist highlight will give you something to do while your child makes decisions about where things will go. In a few hours, he will have had time to do some unpacking and, with luck, meet a roommate or the neighbor across the hall. Parents are usually relieved when they come back after a break and see that their child is feeling more comfortable and confident.

You can offer to take your child out for a meal or make a run to the store for forgotten items, but let him decide if he wants to go. Some students are not ready to say good-bye yet and will appreciate time with their parents to think through the next steps. Others will refuse any suggestion to get back into the car. Either way, it is hard for students to consider this as a family day.

If you have traveled cross-country to bring your child to school, you may be planning to spend a few days in town before heading back. Your student, however, is not likely to have the time or the inclination to fit your plans into her schedule. What's more, if she arranges her meals and spends her free time with you, she will miss opportunities to meet other students and to start exploring campus, which she needs to do during the first few days at college.

Eventually, you will have to go home. Our residential life director bluntly tells parents, "You can't live here. And I'm sorry, but there is no magical time when leaving gets any easier."

Your child will be grateful if you avoid sentimental farewells in front of the roommates. Most students find this step less embarrassing if they walk their parents to the car to say good-bye. All you need to say can be summed up in a few words: "I'm proud of you—I love you." If you are convinced you won't be able to drive for all the tears, just go a few blocks until you're out of sight and park the car for a while.

On the way home, take some time to celebrate your own success—you have reached a family milestone. Buy a book you've been meaning to read, treat yourself to a bouquet of flowers, stop for that hour-long hike you skipped on the way to campus, or just go home and take a long, hot bath. You deserve some self-indulgence. Within forty-eight hours, though, check back with your student.

Some parents think that the "distance" their student needs when he begins college means they should wait for the child to make the first phone call. They make an effort not to call or write until their student does. Although your child probably does not want you to call every night, and he certainly does not want to hear daily reports about how lonely you are, he does want to know you're thinking about him. One student, Lissa, remembers that her roommate's mother sent short e-mail notes every few days and sent a package of cookies or brownies once a week for the first month. Lissa's own mother always sounded happy to receive a call from her daughter, but she made a point of saying that she would not be an interfering mother and call all the time. One day, though, Lissa told her, "I have to say—I'm beginning to feel a little neglected here! Randi's mom sends cookies all the time, and she says she's willing to adopt me. I'm about ready to take her up on the offer."

No matter how glad they were to see their parents leave on move-in day, very few students object to receiving a letter or package from home every now and then.

THE COMPLAINT DEPARTMENT

College viewbooks and compact disks—the colorful recruiting materials that every school mails out to prospective applicants—capture the idealized image we all have of campus life: golden autumn days with students strolling arm in arm past red-brick buildings; a group of smiling young men and women studying together around a library table; fans decked out in school sweatshirts at a basketball game; a student gazing into a microscope under the attentive eye of a bearded professor.

While nearly all students will have moments that resonate with those photographs, they will also have bouts of homesickness, impossible homework assignments, and days when absolutely nothing goes right.

The first days at college usually turn out to be a relief for new students. Things are not nearly as bad as they feared—people are pretty nice, the dorm room isn't as cramped as it seemed that first day, and when a problem arises, the student manages to cope. There is an almost unreasonable happiness to be found in plugging in the phone and discovering it actually works. A huge sense of accomplishment comes from figuring out how to use the college ID card to be admitted to the cafeteria.

Before long, though, the joy fades. Fall semester for freshmen is a roller-coaster ride of ups and downs. With the transition to college, nearly every aspect of students' lives changes. Although they come to school expecting new experiences, they often don't take into account the impact of all that they will encounter.

- They will almost never be alone. In a residence hall, they may share a room with two or more people, and they will almost certainly share a bathroom—in some cases with twenty people.
- There's no accounting for what will drive them crazy. Using the shower after someone else, washing dishes in the bath-

room sink, or the lack of two-ply toilet paper may prove to be far more annoying than a roommate's alarm clock or country music from across the hall.

- There is no such thing as a quiet meal. Even if they like the food, the multiple scents, sights, and sounds of a crowded dining hall become oppressive as a three-times-a-day routine.
- Despite all the activity surrounding them, there will be times of loneliness.

When the going gets tough, the tough call home. Parents will hear complaints about roommates, food, homework assignments, and instructors. During the first month or two of school each year, I frequently receive early morning phone calls from exhausted mothers who couldn't get back to sleep after a 1 A.M. conversation with their student.

"She called in the middle of the night, and she was so depressed. I don't know if I should bring her home or tell her to stick it out."

"He hates it there. He doesn't seem to have any friends. Maybe it was a mistake to send him so far away for college."

Parents feel terrible when their child is unhappy. In most cases, however, after your daughter purged all her frustration, she hung up the phone and went to bed feeling much better. Or after your son unloaded all his misery onto you, he saw his neighbor on the way to the vending machine and spent an hour talking about video games. In the meantime, you don't know that your child feels better. He doesn't call you back the next day to say the problem is solved. And if you call the next night but get no answer, you only worry more.

When your student calls to complain, he is not expecting you to solve the problem. If you offer advice, he will most likely assure you that your solution is unreasonable or impossible. You may suggest that a conversation with the professor will clarify the requirements for an upcoming project, and your student will tell you that it is impossible to talk to this professor—she has office hours only from 8 to 9 A.M., when your son has another class, which he absolutely cannot miss. This instructor would never agree to talk to him outside of her posted office hours. And what's more, not one person in the class has ever been able to talk to this instructor.

Your student is calling you because he needs sympathy. Life is more challenging than ever before, and all this problem solving is hard work. He feels awful, he is recognizing that he probably caused or at least contributed to his problems, and now he must make an effort to fix things. Talking through the issue is part of the review process that allows him to understand how the situation came about. After he has vented his frustration, he will be ready for the next step: figuring out a solution.

By listening, you are providing your student with what he needs. You can't tell him what to do, and it will not help to ask why he let the problem develop, but you can ask some useful questions about moving toward a solution: "What do you think you can do now?" "Do you know of anyone who might be able to help?" "Is there any place you can find some information on this problem?"

He still may argue with your suggestions, but you have done your part: you've given him some possibilities to think about. Your child learns valuable lessons by going through the steps. He learns about the culture and the systems of the college as he finds his way toward a solution. Best of all, he gains confidence that he can make it in this new world.

STARTING OUT STRONG

The opening days of college set the patterns that can mean the difference between success and failure. The routines that students establish during the first weeks tend to last at least through the first semester, sometimes longer. The patterns they form become a part of who they are and how they interact with the campus. Students who spend September weekends partying will probably look for a party every weekend in October and November. The commuters who hurry home after class every day during the first few weeks may never carve out their own niche on campus or form a study group with other students.

College students are usually in class only 15 to 18 hours a week. Compared to a high school schedule, college might seem like a vacation. The expectation, however, is that for every hour a student is in class, another two to three hours should be spent studying. A class schedule of 15 credit hours, then, should translate into a weekly time commitment of 30 to 45 hours outside of class. Students who revel in the free time and postpone writing their papers until the last minute, or who pull all-nighters to cram for their final exams, will not be as successful as they could have been.

It's not only what students are doing, but how they are relating to the campus, in the first few weeks that makes a difference. Too many students turn to their computers for a social life, sacrificing real-life, real-time companionship. Computer games consume hours of free time and turn into obsessions. Students stay up long into the night, communicating with high school friends or chatting with faceless icons in cyberspace, and they fail to meet the people who live across the hall. They even use computers to fight with their roommates. A residence hall adviser in Wisconsin found out that two students on his hall had been feuding for months. The roommates literally did not speak to one another. They would each sit at their desks on opposite sides of the room and send vitriolic messages back and forth. The hostility—and the silence—in the room was oppressive.

Listen as your child describes campus life during the first few weeks of classes. By the sixth week, students should be talking about course work, accomplishments and challenges, instructors, and new friends. Commuter students should be spending the majority of their day on campus, doing homework, and meeting with their instructors or other students. Residential students should be dedicating blocks of time to studying, not trying to read a few pages in the ten minutes before class. All students should be making connections on campus.

If your child continues to talk exclusively about friends from home, or if the focus of her conversations relates only to the social activities on campus, it's probably time for a serious discussion about educational goals and adjustment to college. At least one class should be challenging enough to talk about; at least one instructor should be engaging enough to merit attention; at least one paper or test should be worth telling you about. Even if your child is mostly just complaining, as long as she's talking about college, she is becoming involved.

COLLEGE CULTURE SHOCK

Freshmen are subjected to every possible warning and tidbit of advice about safety, security, and student success. Residence hall staff talk about fire drills, cooking regulations, night-time security procedures, and alcohol policies. Academic staff lecture on time management, study skills, and the value of setting up study groups. Student affairs staff stop by to talk about getting involved on campus, developing leadership skills, and making smart choices about finances and health.

Meanwhile, there are new words and new traditions that students are expected to somehow know—the University of Michigan freshman is confused when his classmate tells him to meet him in the "fish bowl" between classes. At Wake Forest, the student is supposed to know when to show up for "rolling the quad." And college presents first-year students with challenges far beyond the classroom. The suburban student who goes to school in a big city can't imagine life without a car. The city dweller who goes to a small rural college is surprised to find there is no bus service—so how do you get to a store to buy shampoo? The farm kid from Nebraska is puzzled to see people carrying umbrellas on her California campus. "Do people really use umbrellas?" she wonders. "I thought that was something only the British do, or characters in books." Where she comes from, if it rains, you stay indoors, drive wherever you're going, or wear a hat.

New information of all kinds is firing in from every direction, and hardly any of it is hitting its mark. First-year students are not looking for advice or wisdom, traditions, or new concepts; they're looking for friends. But friend-making is one of those skills no one ever thought to teach them.

Friendships, in their experience, just happen. If they grew up in a small community, their parents knew the families of all their friends. Neighborhood schools or private schools usually draw students who share similar backgrounds, and most of their friends have been much like themselves. Even those from large city schools with considerable diversity had friends from a limited social circle—people they knew from their neighborhood, church, or "friends of friends." When they started dating in high school, they already knew something about the person they were going out with, or they at least knew someone who could provide some information.

In college, they don't have family references for the people they're meeting. They have to figure out not only who will be fun and interesting, but also who will be trustworthy. In their urgency to have a friend or a lover, many students make poor choices and then don't know how to break off a relationship.

Students of color might find themselves feeling particularly isolated. Even at a large university that boasts of its 25 percent minority enrollment, an African-American freshman might be the only nonwhite on his floor of the residence hall; a Hmong student may be the only person of color in the 200-seat lecture hall during psychology class. Most colleges have culture-based student groups to give students of color a place to meet, receive support on campus, and celebrate diversity. Although most students will settle in comfortably in time, initial feelings of difference and separation can be particularly difficult in the first few weeks of college.

Everyone wants to have friends and be accepted. Lonely students seeking companionship are vulnerable to predatory religious groups as well as seemingly innocent campus-sponsored student groups that promise camaraderie but then require proof of commitment. Initiation ceremonies and hazing by athletic teams, social organizations, or even the college band sometimes demand that students perform humiliating acts—even deadly behaviors—all in the name of fun and friendship.

Friendship: True or False?

Most college students develop friendships that last a lifetime. Some will meet their future partners. As students experience the revelations that come with a college education, in the classroom and out, they come to treasure the people who share those moments with them

The friends they make can be the most positive—or the most damaging—influence of their college years. Students are vulnerable to bad relationships when they are lonely or homesick, when they have recently broken up with a boyfriend or girlfriend, when they are bored, and when they are struggling academically or financially. The following information, which compares the difference between true and false friends, can be adapted to evaluate social and religious organizations as well.[1]

True Friends

- *True friends take time for you and listen to you.* Your thoughts and opinions are important to them, even if they disagree with your ideas. They are not hurtful about expressing differences.
- *True friends encourage relationships with family and other friends.* They are not jealous or possessive. They are interested in meeting your family and friends.
- *When something goes wrong, true friends want to work through the problems with you.* They can explain why they are upset, and they can acknowledge their responsibility in the problem.
- *True friends support your goals and encourage your success.* They believe in you and want you to do well.
- *True friends are people you feel safe with.* They do not ask you to bend the rules, and they respect your values and concerns.
- *True friendships develop and grow over time.* Instant friendships can end as quickly as they begin. Friends take the time to know one another well.

False Friends

- *False friends demand all your attention and are jealous of your other friends.* They question your loyalty to them, and they become anxious or upset if they don't know where you are.
- *For false friends, the relationship is all about them.* They expect you to be there for them, to do what they want, and to devote yourself to them. Your thoughts and opinions are important only if they conform to their ideas.

- *False friends don't think anything is their fault.* When things go wrong, it's your fault or someone else's. They are never wrong, and they are never responsible for problems.
- *False friends become more controlling as time goes by.* You cannot provide enough attention, and you are asked for more and more proof of your devotion.
- *False friends live by their own rules.* They may push the limits of the law, have financial problems, or use drugs and alcohol dangerously. They force you to do things you don't want to do, and they become angry if you challenge them.
- *False friends want too much, too soon.* When you're with them, you feel like things are out of control. If you feel that something is wrong, you're probably right.

As important as it is to be cautious about friendships, parents also should stress that "different" does not equate with "bad." Except for the smallest private schools, most colleges and universities will introduce your student to a world of new ideas, new religions, new cultures. Initially, all the differences can be fascinating. Students between the ages of eighteen and twenty-two are receptive to learning, and they are in an environment that supports them as they open their minds to new people and new experiences.

In time, some of the differences may begin to feel like challenges to their own background and beliefs. When students come across ideas that contrast with their family's values, they have to make some decisions: Should they accept or reject these new ideas? And how should they deal with the people who preach them?

The black-and-white, right-or-wrong perspectives that worked for students in the past are countered by shades of gray. They almost hate to admit that what is wrong in some circumstances might be acceptable in others. Most students learn how to choose what they will accept and make allowances for what they cannot. College students as a whole not only accept diversity, but embrace it. Ideally, they will recognize that they are part of an exciting and energizing community. The fact that they are learning something new every day is proof that they're moving forward with their lives.

MEANWHILE, BACK AT HOME

Just as your child is learning a lot about himself during these first weeks of college, you are learning new things about yourself and the rest of the family.

Thea's parents expected life to be quieter after she left for college, and they knew they would miss her—she was the family storyteller and drama queen. Every night at dinner, she had at least one tale to tell, and she could stretch out a description of her day and all its woes through the entire meal.

What they didn't expect was that their younger daughter would become so difficult after Thea left. At fifteen, she was, they thought, past that challenging adolescent stage. Instead she seemed to have a breakdown at every meal, storming out of the room before they finished eating.

Thea was the lightning rod in her family. As issues arose, she could draw attention away from the problem and toward her. With Thea at college, that tension had nowhere to go. The family was going through a significant adjustment, and her sister's behavior was just one of the results.

Family structures and patterns develop based on *all* members of the household. When one person leaves, it's not just the physical presence, or the humor, or the affection that is missed. It's also the role that that person plays in the family.

Every family develops new patterns when a child leaves home. With only one or two people gathering for dinner, it might seem unnecessary to set the dining room table and have a formal meal. If you're running late, it may be easiest to allow the only child still at home to eat in front of the TV.

Some of the changes will feel like a gift. You don't have to share bathroom time with as many people. The phone interrupts meals less frequently. You get your car back, or at least you don't lie awake every Friday night waiting to hear your daughter come in the front door. The brother or sister still living at home is receiving extra attention; morning schedules are less hectic; if your last child just left home, you and your partner can talk about sex any time, even at the dinner table.

On the other hand, without your children as the center of your relationship, you may find yourself feeling lost and alone. For many seemingly stable families, a child's college years coincide with marriage problems. You may discover that all you have talked about together for the past five years is your kids. The dissonance in the household caused by a child's departure results in one parent's seeking change while the other clings to stability.

It is common to "mourn" for a while when a child leaves home, and it's not entirely coincidental that parents' midlife crises correspond to their children's college years. You might even feel a touch of envy for what your child is experiencing. As you begin to see your responsibilities to your child more in terms of financial obligations, you might begin evaluating your beliefs and values, and perhaps you will decide it's time to do something for yourself. Countless parents look at the school their student is attending and say, "I wish *I* could go to college. Someone would fix my meals, I could take any classes I want, I would have no responsibility, and I could have intellectual conversations every day. Why do we waste all this on kids?"

You're stuck with your responsibilities, but you can still

expand your mind. This is the best time in your life to take a class at a local college, devote time to a hobby, concentrate on your career, or pamper your partner. As your new life develops, you need to look for ways to adapt to and create new routines. Depending on your outlook, all the changes in your life might feel a bit daring and exciting or somewhat depressing.

On the other hand, you might be oblivious to any particular differences at all until the first time your student comes home for the weekend, expecting everything to be the same, and points out the new routines. "We *always* have pancakes for Saturday breakfast. Why are there cereal boxes on the table?"

When students come home and find life even a little different, they feel unsettled. This is partly because they did not have a voice in the changes and partly because they don't know how these adjustments will affect them. They rarely object to new living room furniture, as long as you save the comfortable old couch for their first apartment. There are limits to what feels like progress and what feels like an attack on their territory. They still don't want you to change their bedroom into your exercise room. Personal space is sacred, at least until your child gets his own apartment.

Students find comfort in returning to the familiar, and they rely on the stability of "family," but they don't really expect everything to remain as it always has been. They'll let you know they are surprised—maybe even disappointed—at any changes. But they adjust. They go back to school and tell their friends, with pride and amusement, that their mother signed up for ski lessons, their father took a first-ever trip to New York City, or Grandpa enrolled in computer classes at the community college.

Mini-Calendar of the First Six Weeks

Move-In Day

A tough day for families. Students are tense, excited, scared. Parents are on edge; if anything goes wrong, they may find themselves reacting more strongly than they would expect. *Advice for parents:* Tell your child you love and trust her, and you have great confidence that she will be fine.

Week 1

Students establish routines as a way to adapt to change. Social acceptance is usually their first priority. Students react strongly to disappointments or problems. This may be the first time they have had to identify problems and find solutions entirely on their own. They will complain, but they usually manage to adjust. Every accomplishment feels like a significant victory. *Advice for parents:* Talk to your child at least once during the first week; enjoy the excitement, and acknowledge the disappointments.

Week 2

Students may go overboard with new freedoms. They figure out that attendance is not taken in classes, and they decide not to go. They realize that they have two hours between their lecture and their lab, and they spend the time with friends in a coffee shop. They see other students decorating their rooms, and they spend a small fortune on posters and pillows. *Advice for parents:* Listen for clues that your child might be making poor decisions. Affirm the good choices and talk about priorities.

Week 3

A mix of comfort and uneasiness confuses students. They have established a routine, and they no longer feel "new." They become extremely close to friends they have just met. They can't believe they've only known these people a couple of weeks. On the other hand, students are frustrated that there is clearly so much they don't know yet about college. They think that everyone is looking at them and thinking, "Obviously clueless. Must be a freshman." Any mistakes feel like proof they don't belong. *Advice for parents:* Tell your child you believe in her.

Week 4

Students who have not yet gone home begin to want a weekend away from college. The intensity of it all has become exhausting, and they're worn out. They begin to see things from a slightly different perspective—the gregarious, outgoing friend they met the first week of school starts to seem a bit shallow; the quiet, cynical person next door might not be so bad after all; and they get tired of roommates. *Advice for parents:* Listen to complaints, but don't try to fix things. Suggest that rather than come home for the weekend, your child can stay at school and spend some extra time sleeping and studying over the weekend. The standard recommendation is that students should stay at school until Thanksgiving break.

Weeks 5 and 6

Students begin to react to disillusionment. College turns out not to be everything they had imagined, and they have to admit that some of their initial choices were poor. Typically, students either confront their challenges and make improvements, or they confirm their original patterns. Students will continue to cycle through frustration and action throughout the first semester, deciding to drop bad habits or bad friends or concluding, "Since this is what college is, maybe I'm not cut out for college." *Advice for parents:* Talk with your child about the good decisions you have seen him make during the first few weeks of school. Let him know there is still time to make improvements.

QUICK TIPS FOR STUDENTS

- The first day of school, you are *not* the only one who doesn't know what's going on. All freshmen are scared and confused.

- If your parents are irritable on move-in day, that's because they're nervous, too. Your going to college is almost as big a change for them as it is for you.

- The patterns you set in the first week of college are the ones you will tend to follow for a long time. Make sure they're good ones. When you find yourself doing the same thing every day, ask yourself, "Is this a routine I want to continue?"

- Get up, get out, and get involved. Turn off the computer, meet the people across the hall and on the floor above yours. Say hello to the person sitting beside you in every class. Talk to the person next to you as you go through the cafeteria line. Someday, one of those people will say, "I am so glad you came up to me that first time!"

- The way you feel today is not how you'll feel tomorrow. The first weeks of school bring lofty highs and deep lows. You will have days when you're not at all sure you're at the right school, but you'll also have days when you know you are doing just fine. Remember the good days so you can draw on them during the rough times.

- Be willing to rethink your choices. You can drop friends who don't turn out to be what you expected; you can change majors; you can ask forgiveness for doing something stupid. The best part of being a freshman is that for a whole year, you can say, "I'm still trying to figure things out."

- For commuters, setting classes as your top priority is even harder than for students who live in a dorm. Spend your free time on campus, make a space there for yourself, and start to think of college as your "real life."

CHAPTER 3

No More Notes on the Refrigerator

Parenting from a Distance

You and your child have been working through issues surrounding independence for years. At least once during high school, and certainly during that senior summer, your child must have declared, "You can't tell me what to do; I'm not a little kid anymore." It's true. You really *can't* tell your college-age child what to do. You have much less direct control, but you do still have influence, and you will continue to care deeply about how he is and whether he is safe, comfortable, and happy. For the next four years, you will be parenting your student from a distance, which requires greater trust from you and greater responsibility from your child.

If parents have studied psychology, they will recognize that the steps they go through in transferring responsibility to their child track Maslow's Hierarchy of Needs. The psychologist Abraham Maslow said that certain basic physiological needs must be met (food, drink, and sleep) before we can move on to satisfy additional needs. When we are confident that we have sufficient food and drink and a place to sleep, we will turn to ensuring protection against danger. With a sense of security, we're ready to seek friendship and a sense of belonging, then self-respect and self-esteem, and finally self-actualization and an outlet for creativity.

The college-selection and leaving-home stages replicate Maslow's Hierarchy, with parents seeking assurance that all their child's needs will be met. Parents insist on being involved as their student reviews residence hall choices to make sure that their child will have a comfortable place to live. They want to know about meal plans so they can be assured their child will eat well. On Move-In Day, they check to ensure the safety precautions are all in place. They flick light switches, make sure there is a smoke alarm, ask about the sprinkler system, and take a close look at the lock on the door.

When parents go home after settling their student into the dorm, they may be ready to transfer the basic responsibilities to their student, but they will require ongoing assurance that their child is safe, secure, and happy. It is not quite enough for them to know that they have provided for room, board, and safety; they want to be sure their student is making the right choices about those basic needs. They will continue to ask, "Are you eating all right? Is your room OK? Are you getting enough sleep? Are you making sure to walk with someone when you're out after dark?" Students hate the questions, but parents feel compelled to hear the answers. In reality, the question is "Can you take care of yourself?"

With those essential needs met and confirmed, parents' worries turn to whether their student is making friends and fitting in to campus life. After comfort and safety issues, parents of freshmen express the most concern about their child's social adaptation. "Are you getting along with your roommates? Have you joined any groups? Do you have any friends?"

By the sophomore or junior year, parents again begin to wonder, has my child chosen the right field of study? It's not too late to change majors, is it? Next they will question whether this major can provide an actual career. Will she get a job? Is he doing the right things to get into graduate school? And finally, during the senior year, has this whole college experience been worthwhile?

Although college parents work their way up this Pyramid of Protection, they also routinely return to that baseline of basic needs. When their third-year student moves into his first apartment, they will worry about whether he can make his own meals and how safe the neighborhood is. Indeed, it may not be enough to *hear* that the apartment is safe and there is food in the cupboard; parents may need to see the evidence. Then they will move up the pyramid again and look for reassurance about the people he has selected as roommates and whether he will remember to pay the bills on time.

Comparison between Maslow's Hierarchy of Needs and the College Parent's Pyramid of Protection

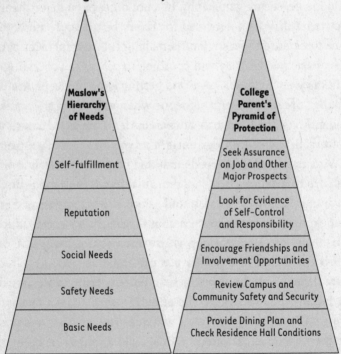

Maslow's Hierarchy of Needs	College Parent's Pyramid of Protection
Self-fulfillment	Seek Assurance on Job and Other Major Prospects
Reputation	Look for Evidence of Self-Control and Responsibility
Social Needs	Encourage Friendships and Involvement Opportunities
Safety Needs	Review Campus and Community Safety and Security
Basic Needs	Provide Dining Plan and Check Residence Hall Conditions

Adapted from Abraham Maslow, *The Farther Reaches of Human Nature* (New York: Viking, 1971).

"I'M PAYING THE BILLS! WHAT ARE *MY* RIGHTS?"

You're paying thousands of dollars for tuition, but you can't get a copy of your daughter's grades. You handed over all your personal financial information to the college, but you can't see your son's billing statement. Your sophomore was ordered to move out of the residence hall, but the hall director won't tell you why.

An eighteen-year-old college student is considered an adult—except, of course, for all those circumstances when he is not. If you think this is confusing for you, look at it from your child's viewpoint. The college tells him he is an adult and he is responsible for his own behavior and all of his debts. Then they remind him that he can't drink legally until he's twenty-one. His financial aid is based on his parents' income until he reaches the age of twenty-four. And at any time, his parents can show up with a tax statement proving he is financially dependent on them, and suddenly all his rights are gone.

Throughout a child's elementary and high school years, the federal Family Educational Rights and Privacy Act (FERPA, also known as the Buckley Amendment) grants parents access to their child's educational records and protects those records from public scrutiny. When students enroll in college, however, their records become their own. Grades, financial information, disciplinary action, and even the number of credits a student is taking are all considered confidential. Financial aid officers, registration staff, medical personnel, and psychologists will not release information to parents unless they receive written permission from the student. Residence hall staff and judicial affairs professionals will encourage students to talk to their parents about behavior issues, but they won't discuss problems with the family unless the student agrees.

A few years ago, FERPA was modified to allow, but not require, colleges to notify parents about violations of student conduct codes. Not all colleges have adopted these parent notification policies, but many schools will now tell parents if a student violates campus alcohol or drug rules. Other student records continue to be protected.

The obvious complaint—and we hear it every day—is "I'm the parent, and I am paying for my child's education. Why can't I get any information?" You can, but only with your child's permission or by submitting your federal income tax forms, showing that you claim your child as a dependent. No matter where their child attends college, parents can have access to student records if their child signs a release form. At some schools, release forms now are routinely distributed to freshmen at orientation. Because incoming freshmen tend to sign any papers they receive, new students often don't realize they are surrendering some of their rights to privacy.

Although the time may come when you wish the college would hand over your student's records, most parents agree that there are good reasons to honor student privacy. A student should have the right to prevent a noncustodial parent from receiving personal contact information; colleges and universities do not know if the person seeking information is truly the parent; stalking and harassment can and do result from access to personal information. Colleges and universities will not assume that every family is loving and caring, because, unfortunately, some are not.

INFORMATION IS POWER

As parent notification policies and release forms have become more common, parents and college administrators have expressed surprise that the voice of protest from students has been quieter than they expected. Today's students seem to recognize the high cost of a college education, and they don't want to squander their parents' investment. Moreover, this generation of students is accustomed to turning to their parents for guidance, and they continue to want family support. As first-year students, they are overwhelmed by the decisions they are required to make, as well as the potential for making the wrong choices.

Although a freshman might acknowledge that there are good reasons for his parents to see his student records, parents still are likely to encounter defiance from their student when it comes down to precisely which information they can see. Your son will be happy to have you receive and pay the tuition bill, but he wishes the bill would not reflect that he's taking only 10 credits this semester. Your daughter is happy to show you her grade reports when she's earning A's and B's, but she won't want you to see the report that includes an Incomplete in astronomy. She would like you to cover the co-payments for her medical appointments, but she doesn't want you to know about the 2 A.M. emergency room visit last weekend. You feel as if you are always hearing only half the story.

To most parents, the boundaries their child constructs seem less like clear fences than like a complicated maze. Your child will allow you to come just so far into his life, but the moment you ask about his new girlfriend or the state of his finances, he'll put up an impenetrable barrier: "There's really nothing to talk about! Oh—I think I have another phone call. Sorry, I have to go."

If you back up and wind your way down a less direct path, you might find that he's not only telling you about his girlfriend, he's asking you to stop by the dorm sometime soon to meet her. He may not tell you the balance on his credit card, but he might ask if you think it makes sense to have a debit card instead of a checking account.

For families of commuter students, the confrontations are more challenging. Students are trying to become independent, but they are living at home. Parents can hardly avoid asking questions—"Will you be home for dinner?" "Do you need the car tonight?" The questions seem logistical to you, but your child interprets them as interference.

Since you are not part of your child's college life, most of the time, you don't even know what to ask. When you do know the questions, you don't know when to ask them. And you just can't understand how your most innocent comments seem to inspire such negative reactions.

Let's look at what goes on in a student's mind when you ask a simple, seemingly noninvasive question like "What did you do this weekend?"

To begin, a weekend might include everything from Thursday evening through Sunday, and your daughter probably was busy with dozens of different activities during that time. Now that you've asked about it, she will have to sort through a long list and decide what to tell you. She figures you would be more impressed to hear that she spent five hours studying on Sunday afternoon than that she went shopping Friday evening, or that she was out with friends all day Saturday. She considers that she probably should tell you she overspent her clothing budget, but she doesn't really want to hear that same old sermon about money management. She already knows she should be more careful with her finances, so she gives herself a little reproof on your behalf, skips over all of Friday's activities, and decides she doesn't want to talk about Saturday or Sunday either.

"Nothing much" is her answer. "I'm doing laundry tonight, and actually, I better go get my clothes out of the dryer now so someone else can use it."

Nevertheless, there are things you need to know, such as when tuition is due. Or when spring break is scheduled. Or if it really makes sense for your son to be taking three physical education classes and something called "Self Actualization."

Counselors recommend that parents ask questions that cannot be answered with a simple yes or no. At the same time, you don't want to appear to be prying for too much personal information. Once your student starts talking and is convinced that you are listening, not judging, he will share as much as feels comfortable to him. Some ideas for conversation starters:

- Ask open-ended questions that show interest in your child's experiences, such as "How does your Spanish class compare with the language classes you took in high school?" "How much variety is there in the food they serve in the cafeteria?" "What is there to do on campus on the weekends?" "Now that you've been in school for a while, is there anything from home that you want me to send?"

- If your child doesn't seem to want to talk, don't ask about her silence; instead *you* can carry the conversation for a while. Talk about things that you know interest her. If she participated in high school sports, tell her how the team is doing and mention some of the athletes she played with. Talk about the family pet.

- Often, parents are so intrigued by their student's new life, they forget that their child still needs to know at least a little about what is happening at home. Describe the repairs you're having done on the car or mention that you spent the morning doing laundry, vacuuming, and washing floors. These reports remind your child that not *everything* in his life is changing. Also tell him about anything new that he will encounter when he comes home—like the new toaster, or the new tile you're having installed in the bathroom.

- Avoid judging. Students are sensitive to any hints of disappointment or criticism. If you need to ask about finances, student records, or other specific information, keep that part of the discussion separate from the personal conversation, and be clear about your expectations. "It sounds like you're doing well, and I'm proud of you. Before we hang up, we need to get a little business done. To keep you on my health insurance policy, my personnel office has to have a statement from the college saying you're taking at least 12 credits this semester. I need to have it by the fifteenth of the month, and they say that students usually get those forms from the registrar's office."

In the best of situations, your child will give you the information you need, even if the message is not all that you might wish. Because students don't want to disappoint their family, though, they will work hard to prevent their parents from seeing poor grade reports, finding out that they did something foolish, or hearing that they are in serious trouble. To a young adult trying to attain independence, keeping bad news from Mom or Dad is a way to avoid the lectures and control they have been trying to escape. Sometimes students will be vague about what's happening in their lives, and sometimes they will flat-out lie.

When you hear something from your student that doesn't seem to ring true, consider whether there is something he or she may not want to acknowledge. If your child tells you that the college doesn't provide transcripts, or that the school doesn't post grades, you probably have a clue that there are academic difficulties. If you suddenly hear about an unexpected "$100 registration fee," this may be an indication that your child has some kind of expense she does not want you to know about.

A discussion at the start of the college experience, plus occasional follow-up conversations, can establish expectations about what kind of information you will share and which topics can be considered private or discretionary. Your student probably will not want to share details of every quiz or expenditure, and you will not hear about every party or date, but parents are justified in asking for general information on grades, the social scene, health issues, and bottom-line financial balances.

If you don't show an interest in your student's education, she will think you don't value how hard she is working. If you show too much interest, she will think you are infringing on her privacy. Parents struggle with the fine line they must walk, but most agree the path is smoothest when they express frequent admiration for their child's efforts. When students see that their parents use information to provide support rather than assert control, they end up providing information because they *want to* rather than because they *have to*.

"HOW DO I GET SOME ANSWERS AROUND HERE?"

It takes time to sift through the new communication processes when students start college. A parent's expectations about how and when information will be shared are rarely the same as the student's.

When Marcy's family said good-bye after moving her into the freshman residence hall, they told her to be sure to call and let them know how she was doing. They expected to hear from her within a day or two. The third day passed with no word, so Marcy's father called her. He was anxious to talk to his daughter, but his mood turned to irritation when Marcy's voice-mail recording brightly announced "You know who this is, and you know what to do. Wait for the beep." Stifling his annoyance, he did his best to sound nonchalant as he left a message saying that he hoped things were going well and asking her to call when she had a chance.

She still had not called home by the end of the week, and on Friday her parents began phoning every couple of hours. Obviously, she was not in class every minute. They went from irritation to anger—was she even checking her voice mail? How irresponsible was she, refusing to call home like this? Then they blamed the college—her voice mail must not be working. Maybe her phone didn't work at all. The dorm should provide some alternate way to get in touch with students. Next, fear set in. Was she all right? Had she left school, and was she afraid to tell them? Did *anyone* know where she was?

When her parents finally reached her, Marcy couldn't understand why they seemed so upset. "I got your messages, but I've been busy. I would have called if something was wrong," she said. "Am I supposed to talk to you every day? I really didn't have anything to say. Everything's fine."

Throughout high school, the only times Marcy phoned her parents were when she needed a ride or if she found that she would be later than expected. She had never called home "just to talk." Marcy thought that she would call home if she had a specific question or a problem. It didn't occur to her that a quick five-minute phone call the day after she started school would have mattered so much to her parents. She wasn't homesick for them yet, so she didn't share the urgency to make contact.

"I'm not going to tell you everything that goes on in my life," she said. "I don't want to have to come up with a weekly Marcy report."

Marcy's parents explained that while they wanted to know if their daughter had any problems, they also wanted to hear the good news. Most important, they simply needed to hear her voice and know that she was all right.

TECHNOLOGY: HIGH TECH, LOW TOUCH

Communication between students and their parents is not the same as it was a generation ago. When you first left home, you probably scheduled a collect call to Mom and Dad at a time when you knew they would be home to accept the charges. Or you waited to place the call during less expensive "evening and weekend" hours. Now, however, students pull out their cell phones as they're walking between classes. Your child may be talking to you on the way to an exam, and you might get another call minutes after she turns in her test. Technology—particularly cell phones, e-mail, and instant messaging—has dramatically affected the relationship between parents and students.

The speed of communication means that students don't spend much time processing information before they call home. Parents hear the news when it is still raw and emotional. When your student uses his cell phone to call you at work and report that he's standing outside the financial aid office, and he's missing a required form, it will seem like a major crisis to him. Your instinct will be to try to figure out a solution immediately, while he's on the line. If, on the other hand, he had waited to call until seven-thirty that evening, he would have had time to find the form himself or figure out how to deal with the problem. At any rate, the issue would not be complicated by such urgency.

This immediate contact is both a blessing and a curse. Parents and students are communicating more, but technology has also raised expectations. A father knows his daughter has a cell phone; if he calls and gets no answer, he may panic. Students, however, frequently forget to turn on or recharge their cell phones when they're the busiest and happiest.

E-mail brings similar mixed blessings. If a parent sends a message and a response doesn't come within twenty-four hours, she worries. The student, however, may have only skimmed his messages and not read the part where his mother asked him to respond. Maybe he has been doing countless other things and hasn't checked his e-mail in a couple of days. Or maybe he glanced at his list of messages and thought "An e-mail from Mom. I don't have time to write back to her now, so I'll wait and read that one later."

Some parents insert code words into the subject line of e-mail messages when they must have a quick response. One family has agreed that urgent messages will be titled "Respond Now." Another mother says she always gets a reply if she writes "Want money?" in the heading.

"High tech" has some "high touch" benefits as well, though. Students and their parents find that e-mail allows them to say things to each other they could not say in person or over the telephone. The lack of visual cues makes for more personal communication. As they write a message, there are no interruptions and no body language or voice inflections to stop the train of thought. Consequently, e-mail users frequently disclose far more than they would in person, much as a journal writer confides more on paper than she does out loud to a friend. Fathers, especially, are likely to communicate more openly with their child by e-mail.

"I hate talking on the phone," one father said. "I don't chat well, and once I've said whatever it is I'm calling about, I can't think of anything else to say. Then I hear my son's roommates in the background, or the TV is on, and I feel like he's probably got better things to do than talk to me. If I send an e-mail message, I figure he'll read it when he has the time. With a phone call, I feel like I have to have something important to say, but I can send an e-mail if some little thing pops into my mind. Yesterday, I was eating a tuna sandwich at my desk, and I sent him a message saying 'I'm sitting here at work, eating your favorite kind of sandwich, and I'm thinking about you. You're a great kid, and I love you.' I'm not the kind of guy who could ever call and say that to him. In an e-mail, I can."

Parents and students may reveal more through e-mail than they ever had before. The emotion that comes out in e-mails, however, can create unrealistic expectations the next time they see each other in person or talk on the phone. When students come home for a weekend or a school break, families often find that they need a period of adjustment. Patterns of communication don't change overnight. Just because you can write to each other about deep feelings does not mean that you can jump into face-to-face conversations on the same topics.

Multiple technologies create more opportunities for different kinds of communication—a brief e-mail just to let your student know you're thinking of him; a short voice-mail message with the latest news item from home; a lengthy phone call when you know you both have some free time; instant messaging while you're watching the same TV program. Ask almost any student, though, and he'll tell you not to forget the old standby—the U.S. Postal Service. Students may not *write* letters, and they will choose to make a phone call or dash off an e-mail message when they want to communicate with you, but every day as they pass the residence hall desk or the student union mail center, they check their mailboxes, hoping something will be inside. Receiving a card, a letter, or best of all a package is an increasingly rare gift in an electronic world.

IS IT A BAD DAY OR A BIG PROBLEM?

A few weeks after starting college, Leslie called home with a list of complaints. Her classes were much too difficult, she didn't have any close friends at school, the food was awful, and to top it all off, the basketball coach had rebuffed her request to try out for the varsity team.

To Leslie's mother, this sad and angry person did not sound like her daughter. In high school, Leslie was a class officer, a top athlete, and a school leader with a host of friends. Her mother began to worry that the family history of chronic depression might be affecting her buoyant, optimistic child.

Most problems are fleeting, and parent intervention not only is unnecessary, it is also unwanted. In Leslie's case, she was hurt by the basketball coach's rejection of her bid to join the team.

She was embarrassed because she had not realized that all the members of the varsity team were recruited as high school players, and there were no walk-ons at her school. The confrontation was a reminder that she had a lot to learn about how the university worked, and it colored her opinion of the entire school for a couple of days. A week later, though, her physical education instructor happened to mention that there were several intramural basketball squads looking for members. Leslie found the team she needed, and she was fine.

If your student is truly stymied about how to proceed with a problem, tell her to start by asking the closest "authority figure" she can find. It might be her residence hall assistant, her academic counselor, or an instructor. If the first person she asks does not have an answer, tell her to ask someone else. In almost every case, by the time she has talked to three people, she will have a good lead. Someone will direct her to the right office or the best expert.

Parents want their students to tell them what's happening in their lives, but it's not always easy to hear what they're telling you. Some of the clues that parents pick up from their students raise red flags. Your son mentions that he went to a house party Thursday night, and you begin to worry that he is drinking. Your student says, "Everyone else in my French class seems to understand the teacher, but I don't know what she's saying." You fear that she is underprepared for college.

How do you know if your child is heading down the wrong road? How can you support her if she is unhappy? Should you confront your child, or stand back and wait awhile?

Residence hall staff and student services personnel often get calls from parents that begin "I don't want my son to know I'm calling, but can you find out. . . ." In most cases, university staff can't promise to keep your concerns secret. If a residence assistant unexpectedly knocks on the door to check on your child's well-being, your child will guess that someone has alerted the staff person, and you will be the first suspect. Usually, we tell parents that we can make a call or check on the student, but we would prefer to be able to say, "Your parents asked us to look in on you. Is everything OK? Is there anything I might be able to help with?"

If you are looking for advice about your child's behavior, you probably have your own circle of experts to consult. Your friends or coworkers who have students in college can give you an opinion based on their child's experience. A niece or nephew a few years older than your child may be able to offer some useful perspective. A neighbor's child or a recent college graduate who works with you is likely to understand what your student is going through. Talk with the people who know your child and who have some recent insights on campus life.

At some point, it will be you, not your child, who must report some bad news. Over the four or more years that a student is in school, it is almost inevitable that something will change in the family. A grandparent may die, someone in the family could be diagnosed with a serious illness, or the family pet may need to be put to sleep.

During Kari's junior year, her parents decided to divorce. Traveling together from Kansas to Kari's school in Seattle in January to deliver the news was out of the question. They had to tell her over the phone. With both parents on the line, they said they had some difficult information to give her, and they were sorry they had to tell her by phone rather than in person. They told her they had decided to divorce; they had given careful thought to their decision and had tried counseling. They promised to mark all her life celebrations as a family—graduation, marriage, the birthdays of any children she would someday have. Most important, they asked how she was feeling about the information and accepted her tears and anger.

Delivering bad news over the phone, by letter, or by e-mail is at the same time both easier and more challenging than doing so in person. Parents worry if their child doesn't react. "I told my son that his grandfather had had a heart attack and was in serious condition, that he might not live. And my son just said, 'Well, tell him hello for me.' Then he said he had to go study, and he hung up."

Students facing new and difficult situations don't react in predictable ways. If you encourage your child to "talk about it," he'll say something completely inappropriate, or he won't say anything at all. Parents complain, "I don't think he really heard what I was saying." Meanwhile, though, their student has scouted out a friend and repeated every word his parents said with astounding recall. Your child hears you; he just doesn't know how to react.

When you must deliver bad news long-distance, plan on checking back with your child. Give her time to digest the information. Let her know that she can call you if she has any questions, or if she would like to talk. And if she reacts poorly, don't judge her. There is no right response to bad news.

QUICK TIPS FOR STUDENTS

- The college or university you attend regards you as an adult. That means the school will assume you are paying for your education. Unless you make other arrangements, the bills will come to you. If you expect your parents to pay the bills, make sure they receive them! And if they're paying the bills, they will probably want to see your grades.

- Talk to your parents about the kinds of information you will share with them (maybe general information on your financial standing, health issues, overall academic progress, and an overview of the social scene) and what you would prefer to keep private (maybe quiz grades, personal expenses, and details about your dating life).

- If you do not call your parents once a week, at least send a quick e-mail. They need to hear from you and know you are all right.

- Your parents won't be able to solve your problems (although parents sometimes think they can), but you can talk with them about what's bothering you. When you start talking about a problem, you begin to understand what steps you can take to solve it. If you complain to your parents about something, though, be sure to tell them when you're feeling better, too.

CHAPTER 4

Credit Loads and GPAs

Adjusting to College Academics

When parents ask "How is school?" they expect to hear a brief report on a recent paper, midterm grades, or a list of the classes their student will be taking next semester. They probably will not be happy if the response is, "I only had one class yesterday, so I spent two hours at the coffee shop, watched a couple of videos with friends, and played a cool new computer game with the guy down the hall until 2 A.M."

The overarching purpose of college is to learn and to prepare for a career path, and the measure of the college experience is the grade point average. The reality of college, though, is that it is a lifestyle. Academics and out-of-classroom activities blend together for the full college experience. As counselors are fond of pointing out, the most important lesson a first-year college student can learn is how to balance studying, social, and personal time.

Today's students come to campus with little experience in structuring their own schedule. The elements of pre-college life were segmented into major blocks of time. Classes filled six or seven hours a day. Students had only five or ten minutes between classes plus a lunch break to visit with friends. Beyond those breaks, friendships waited until after school or on weekends. Evenings were set aside for homework or extracurricular activities, and personal time was carved out of any open spots between family obligations and chores. Most free time was spent in front of the TV or computer, but it never seemed like quite enough.

Suddenly the student arrives at college, and time spent in the classroom drops from thirty or more hours a week to eighteen or fewer. An 8 A.M. class finishing at nine o'clock might lead into a four-hour break in the middle of the day. A few times a week, the school day may end at two o'clock. An evening class might mean even longer gaps of midday free time and then a return to class after dinner. Every day has its own rhythm, and there is no particular portion of the day designated for homework.

Those students who have led the most organized lives often revel in the opportunity to schedule their own time. Left alone to plan their days, they finally have a chance to listen to music for hours on end, lie in bed and read a novel, or head out to the mall in the middle of the morning to shop. And no one is there to remind them of any obligations.

This freedom comes at the same time students are faced with different teaching and learning methods, higher classroom expectations, the need to make new friends, and greater academic competition than they ever experienced before. It's no wonder the first semester is often disastrous.

ACADEMIC EXPECTATIONS

All his life, Aaron planned to go to the university his parents had attended. The family lived just an hour away from the school, and every year they bought alumni season tickets for football and basketball. As an infant, Aaron was the photogenic baby in the crowd wearing a miniature school sweater, and during high school, most of his wardrobe was made up of T-shirts and caps featuring the college mascot. As a first-semester freshman, Aaron taught all his friends the words to the alma mater, and at football games, he helped the cheerleaders fire up the student section. When he met his parents for dinner after the games, they were delighted to see him feeling so comfortable in the student union and finding his way around all the traditional campus hangouts.

A student earning A minus to B plus in high school, Aaron expected to do well at college, and his parents were confident that he would be successful. They were blindsided when he told them in January that he had been placed on academic probation.

Aaron's parents, who had met as economics majors in the university's competitive business school, thought that Aaron knew his first priority in college should be his coursework. Aaron, however, had seen only the social side of college throughout his life, and it never occurred to him that college might present more difficult academic challenges than he had experienced in high school. When his parents talked about their college experience, they had always focused on their memories of athletic events, dances and parties, and the spring break trip they took together as seniors. Only after learning that Aaron's first semester had been three months of playing did they think to talk to him about the hard work and dedication they had both put into college.

"You know, Aaron," his father said, "we *did* go to parties and games when we were in college, but we treated social activities as our reward for studying all week. And there were a lot of times when we couldn't take time out for fun.

"I still remember how I felt one weekend in my sophomore year when I had to choose between going to the last football game of the season or studying for a macroeconomics test. It was killing me because that was the game that would decide whether or not we were going to the Rose Bowl. But I knew I had to do well on the test because I was right between a B and a C for the course. I had to get an A on the test in order to raise my grade and qualify for the business program the next year.

"I stayed home from the game and spent the morning reviewing everything we had covered all semester. I forced myself to keep studying most of the afternoon and then gave myself the reward of listening to the last quarter on the radio.

"I would have had a good time at the game, but I knew that the course work came first. There are a lot of choices you need to make about the way you spend your time, and when your four years of college are done, you will need a solid education to get you where you want to go."

GOOD INTENTIONS, BAD ADVICE

It's easy to see why freshmen emphasize their social life over academics. After all, for the last year or two, students and their parents were visiting colleges, taking tours of residence halls, walking in the shadows of ivy-covered historic buildings, and being guided through impressive sports facilities. On each tour, they heard about the school traditions, the range of activities and events on campus, and the wonderful friends they would find at college. A wide-eyed teenager could easily pick up the notion that higher education is something like a vacation package. They were shopping for the prettiest location, the best food, and the place that promised the most fun.

Certainly, parents want their children to have fun in college, but they also want their students to use this time well. They try to provide guidance as their child prepares for college, but with every good intention, parents sometimes provide some of the worst possible advice.

In many cases, parents are thinking back to their own college years, trying to help their children avoid the mistakes they made.

They urge their students to select a prestigious major as incoming freshmen, test out of introductory classes, and get all their liberal education requirements out of the way in the first two years. As a result, students end up feeling bored, overextended, and lost in challenging lab classes or vast lecture courses that are beyond their comfort level. They commit to a major that turns out to be a poor fit, but they believe they must stick with the plan.

In his book *Making the Most of College: Students Speak Out,* Harvard professor Richard Light notes that first-year students are happiest when they have a mix of large and small classes. During the first semester, students should take at least one class for fun, Light says. Colleges and universities are supporting this idea by offering freshman seminars, small classes taught by some of the best professors, to connect students at the beginning of their college career with some of the school's top instructors. Unlike large, broad-based introductory lecture classes, seminars focus on a topic and explore it thoroughly, inviting discussion with diverse perspectives. Freshman seminars might offer tips for student success, or they may be cutting-edge science courses on laser technology, an analysis of a presidential campaign during an election year, a study of constitutional law, or a course on happiness. A Minnesota professor teaches "The Color Red" in a freshman seminar that investigates everything from the physical components of the color to the psychological, physiological, and political reactions it inspires.

Light also recommends foreign language courses as a way for students to connect with each other in smaller groups that meet on more frequent schedules. Language classes usually meet four or five days a week, and students are required to speak in class, working in pairs or small groups to practice their conversation skills. Instructors ask students to talk about subjects they know well—family, hometowns, how they celebrate holidays, and what they did over the weekend. Students increase their language skills as they learn new words and try to form logical sentences, and they begin to see that mistakes are not fatal. They get to know more about their classmates through their conversational assignments, and classmates then often register together for the next semester's class, extending their relationship beyond a single semester. An extra bonus is that language classes provide background and incentive for study abroad opportunities later on.

GRADES—THE MEASURE OF SUCCESS?

Parents cannot pick their children's classes, but they still play a significant role in academic planning and achievement. Students who understand their parents' expectations about studying and grades use those guidelines to set their own goals. Because college is an entirely new academic environment, however, high school standards may no longer apply. The perfectionist who has never been satisfied with anything less than an A might find himself in a classroom where the professor believes that a C is a perfectly acceptable grade and a C plus means the student did well. Parents should allow some leeway for slightly lower grades, especially during the first year of college, and promote the concept of "doing your best" rather than "being the best."

Grades alone do not provide a full picture of a student's academic progress, especially during the first year. College work is more intense than most students experienced in high school. It takes time to develop the note-taking and test-taking skills, study habits, and time management ability that college courses require.

The freshman year is a tremendous period of adjustment, and the majority of students will not earn grades that match their high school records. A full grade-point drop is typical for the first semester, meaning that a student who has always earned A's and

B's is likely to earn B's and C's. The second semester should show some improvement, and grades should level off as the student begins to feel more comfortable on campus.

If you notice that poor marks are coming from one area of studies—maybe your son is doing well in English and history, but the math grades are low—it could be that high school preparation in that one area was not sufficient for this college. Perhaps he registered for a higher level course than he should have. Possibly his learning style didn't match the teaching style for the class. A pure lecture course, for example, can be very difficult for students who have always been taught through more interactive practices. The broad-based creative writing style that earned an A in a high school literature class may be judged too unfocused for a college essay. Students who are accustomed to using the Internet as their sole research method might find that their college instructor will accept citations only from "peer-reviewed periodicals," and they don't even know what that means.

Most colleges provide tutoring for students who are struggling with skill-level issues. Although there may be a cost involved, one semester of tutoring can give students a boost not only in the coursework, but also in learning how to study for college-level courses. In addition, disability accommodations are provided for students with documented learning disabilities. Counseling and advising offices offer study skills workshops, writing labs, note-taking techniques, and exam preparation. Students can also ask a librarian to check their research methods as they begin working on their first college paper.

Most new freshmen hear the message "Talk to your instructors!" Unfortunately, that may be difficult advice for a first-year student to follow. Freshmen are trying to appear confident, and one of their greatest desires is to avoid drawing undue attention to any weakness they perceive in themselves. The last thing they want is for their professor to think they don't understand the assignments. If they go into their professor's office, what could they possibly say that would improve their situation? "If I ask questions, I'm just putting him on notice that I am confused." Nevertheless, all the evidence indicates that students who talk to their instructors are the most successful, the most committed to on-time graduation, and the most likely to complete their degree.

Some advisers tell first-year students to ask *any* question of an instructor, even if the student already knows the answer. Conversations and relationships can begin from the most simple or awkward start. Others will tell students to ask a general question, such as "How did you first get interested in this field?" Perhaps an easier (and less ingratiating) method is to complete a homework assignment before the due date and ask the professor to check the paper. Instructors are sympathetic to the freshman who is a little insecure about his homework and who wants to head off problems in advance.

Even the best students will come across a course during their college career that seems particularly challenging—it may require a learning style that's difficult for them, or it may simply not be "their" class. Some students will never be able to pass calculus; the rudiments of organic chemistry might not ever make sense. Sometimes a student just doesn't connect with an instructor. The occasional bad grade is not an indication of serious academic trouble, but a continuing trend of progressively lower grades or an entire semester of below-par performance is a sure sign of a problem.

When students are suffering academically, most parents will demand change. According to students, however, the last thing they need to hear from their parents is "Shape up! Crack down! Get to work!"

"If only it could be that easy!" they moan. "There are a lot of reasons for getting bad grades, and being told to 'crack down' doesn't help."

When poor grades are caused by poor choices—partying too much, sleeping too little, spending too much time socializing—the solutions are self-evident. The student must adjust her lifestyle. The issue then becomes whether she wants to change. Most colleges and universities are intent on providing a good education; their primary goal is not to enforce mature behavior. Neither you nor your student can expect the college to monitor your child's lifestyle and ensure her success if she is not willing to make the effort herself.

There are predictable times throughout a student's academic career when difficulties are most likely to occur. For all students, midterm exams create stress halfway through the semester or quarter. Rarely does a student, even the brightest and most organized, go into midterms feeling entirely prepared and comfortable. For freshmen who have never experienced the stress of college exams, the fears are far worse.

From midterm until the end of the semester, the tension steadily grows. Professors set deadlines for major papers or projects right before or right after Thanksgiving break. As a result, students start the week of Thanksgiving with misgiving, and their worries only increase as they try to find time to pack and make travel arrangements. A few days later, heading back to school after the long weekend, they worry that they made little or no progress on their projects—who can study with family and friends vying for attention? The December days leading toward final exams are stress-filled as students try to balance all their end-of-semester responsibilities. Students have accused colleges of blatant cruelty for scheduling finals at the worst possible time of year—just when they must buy and wrap holiday gifts, pack to go home, clean out the refrigerator, and empty the wastebaskets for pre-break room inspections.

The process repeats itself during spring term. A relaxed and hopeful start to the semester is followed by tense days leading to midterms. Spring break leads into the trauma of project dead-lines. Then, worst of all, final exams come just as warm weather and fresh spring breezes tempt students to abandon their books for last chances at fun with friends before summer separates them.

From year to year, the challenges change. There is sophomore slump, the letdown when students realize that things no longer feel new, different, and exciting. Then second-year students must settle on a major, squelching the dream that they can do any-thing they want. Those who were convinced of their career goals as entering freshmen now are wondering how they can switch to some new interest.

The semester when a student moves from a residence hall into an apartment is a significant adjustment period, and grades often drop. During the final year of college, senior stress hits as stu-dents see the demands of the outside world creeping up on them: "Why did I major in classical civilization? I'm never going to get a job. What was I thinking?"

Times of transition are typically accompanied by academic dif-ficulties, but a drop in grades may also be an indication of per-sonal or social problems. Academic problems can be a symptom of health issues, drinking, or drug dependency. Poor grades may signal problems with roommates or a boyfriend or girlfriend. Students who have been sexually assaulted may be able to pro-ject an outward calm, but their grades suffer as a result of the inner anxieties. Poor grades often accompany financial problems. Any time students are examining their career choice and ques-tioning the direction they have selected, they are likely to suffer lower grades.

As a freshman, Clint made good grades. His C in physics was balanced by an A in English, and the rest of his introductory courses were straight B's. As a sophomore, though, he had trou-ble with his math and science classes, and except for elective classes in film production and script writing, his grades were all C or lower.

Although he had always planned to be a chemical engineer, Clint was realizing that he didn't like the sciences as much as he had expected to. English and film studies classes seemed more engaging, and he found himself putting much more effort into homework for those classes, letting chemistry and physics slide. As much as he enjoyed his "just-for-fun" classes, he was becoming increasingly frustrated with himself as he began to question an engineering future. How could he give up a prosperous career in engineering for a major in film studies? He was afraid that he was letting passion get in the way of practicality.

Like many students, Clint couldn't bear to tell his parents he wanted to change his major. "They'll be so disappointed in me," he said. "I've always told them I wanted to be an engineer, and they're paying so much for me to go to school here. I picked this university because of its engineering program. I probably could have gone someplace else for film studies and saved them a lot of money."

Students are surprisingly reluctant to talk to parents about changing majors. We continually come across students who stay with a major they no longer care about, simply because they can't bring themselves to admit their new interest to parents. Or they change majors but refuse to tell their family. I have even heard parents, looking for their student's name in the graduation program under the "Economics" heading, confused when they see his name under "Astronomy." "Well, this is a mistake," they say. "The program has got him under the wrong major. His degree is in economics . . . isn't it?"

HOW MUCH CAN A PARENT DO?

There are times when parents *should* step into their child's academic life, but those instances are limited. If the student has a serious illness, is severely depressed, or for some other reason is incapable of making appropriate decisions, parents can contact campus staff to discuss their concerns. The classroom relationship is between the instructor and the student, however, and in almost every case, a professor will prefer to talk with the student.

Although parents' influence is limited at the college level, students are not entirely on their own; higher education institutions have strong support services in place for students. At small colleges, staff members know the students and can step in to offer guidance when they see problems developing. At big universities, students may need to ask for help, rather than wait for someone to offer it, but help is available. However, it can be confusing for students to identify precisely the type of help they need or determine where to go for assistance.

Meredith selected a large public university as a contrast to the home schooling of her elementary years and the private school she had attended in high school. The first year, she appreciated the chance to create a new identity for herself in each class. No one knew her from one course to the next, and she was content to remain anonymous. She picked out classes that interested her, although they didn't have much relationship to each other. She was dabbling in a range of fascinating subjects, thrilled with the sheer joy of learning in the midst of a vast sea of students.

By the end of her second year, she was required to declare a major and develop a plan of study for her final two years. She had talked with her academic counselor only once, during freshman orientation, long before classes started, and now she didn't remember the adviser's name. Worse, she had no idea how to find him. Describing to her mother the problems she was having, she complained, "I don't know what I'm supposed to do! They expect you to make these decisions before you can sign up for any more courses, but I don't even know what it means to declare a major—am I supposed to sign some paper or something? And how am I supposed to make plans for the next two years? It's not like I can find a list of what classes will be available two years from now. How do I know this is all going to work out?"

Her mother assured Meredith that there must be someone who could help, but Meredith protested, "You don't know what it's like here! I could ask five people what I'm supposed to do, and every one of them would give me a different answer."

Among the first people a student sees at college is an academic counselor or faculty adviser. The counselor will help in the course selection process to make certain that general education requirements are being fulfilled and progress is being made toward graduation. If the student needs extra preparation before taking a math, science, or writing course, the counselor can talk about which basic-level classes will be most helpful.

Students should be checking with an academic counselor at least once each semester during the first two years to ensure they are taking classes that will count toward a degree. Before students declare a major, they can talk to an academic counselor and a career adviser. Once they declare a major, they should check with the counselor at least once a year to make sure they remain on track for graduation and with the career adviser to plan for life after college.

Unlike the staff in the counseling office back in high school, the academic counselor may not be the person students will turn to for personal advising. Depending on the size of the college or university, a separate counseling program might help with adjustment advice, relationship problems, roommate conflicts, time management skills, and mental health issues. For financial problems, students might go to yet another office to talk with financial aid staff. Job seekers will check with student employment or career advisers. Students who are disputing a grade might consult with a student conflict office, and those who are charged with violating a campus policy might be referred to a judicial affairs office.

For new students, and for their parents, the range of offices and options can be confusing. Moreover, the more that colleges rely on computers for everyday transactions—registration, financial aid, and official college communications are all managed online—the more concerned parents become. "Who's taking care of my kid? Where are the *people*?" they wonder. Although many questions can be answered by e-mail or by directing students to the right Web site, personal contact is still an important part of student services, and it begins with residence hall staff, counselors, and academic advisers.

GRADUATING IN FOUR YEARS—OR MORE

Most parents expect their student to earn an undergraduate degree in four years. Some career-based programs require a fifth year, but the general expectation remains at four. In reality, only about a third of students at public universities graduate in four years. Nationally, just over half of full-time freshmen will receive their degree within five years.[2]

Colleges and universities set up a structure to allow students to follow a formula—typically 15 credits per semester over eight semesters of study—to earn the necessary number of credits to graduate on time. More often than not, though, something will interfere with that plan. An illness, failure to complete a critical paper, or the realization that a class is too difficult might convince a student to withdraw from a class mid-semester. One too many withdrawals can lead to delayed graduation.

During the college review process, the admissions office had looked carefully at Amber's application. Her high school grades were only slightly above average, but she had performed in the school choir, and she was a student council member and class treasurer. The assessment was that she would have to apply herself, but she should be able to succeed at college.

The first semester, she registered for 15 credits, but she dropped her biology lab class after deciding she was "not awake enough at 8 A.M. to be using sharp instruments like scalpels and probes." The second semester, she again enrolled for 15 credits, but her French III instructor urged her to withdraw when she failed the first two quizzes. "Since you didn't take French last semester, you've forgotten a lot of your high school language skills. Start with French II next fall or get some tutoring, and you'll be able to catch up."

Although she completed only 11 credits each of her first two semesters, she still couldn't keep up with her courses, and she ended the year with C's and C minuses.

After talking to her counselor, Amber recognized that she needed to develop better time management and study skills. The study habits that had always worked before were not getting her through her college courses. Cramming for exams might have helped her pass the true-or-false history tests in high school, but the essay exams in freshman political science required a deeper understanding of the material.

Amber's parents began to see that the four-year college plan they had anticipated might not be what was best for Amber. In order to succeed, she would first need to put some time into mastering some of the basic learning skills. A lighter academic load for her sophomore year, supplemented by tutoring and academic counseling, brought her up to speed and improved her grades. She managed to graduate in five years with an acceptable grade point average of 2.8.

By the time they are eighteen, students should be responsible for managing their own course loads and doing their best to stay on track. When they fall behind by a class or two, though, it becomes increasingly easy for students to conclude that graduating in four years is out of the question. They put themselves on a five- or six-year track without considering the extra expense to their parents or to themselves. Parents who are footing the bills, then, are dismayed when they learn that their student expects an extra year or more of support.

As a parent, you can ask for a periodic accounting of progress toward a degree. The number of credits earned is one guide, but more critical is the number of credits still needed to fulfill the requirements. Is the student taking the *right* courses? Just because a student is earning 15 credits per semester does not mean she will graduate in four years with 120 credits. Some of those classes may not count toward graduation. Every college has seniors with excess credits who still cannot graduate. Students must earn a certain number of credits within their major, and they must take a range of courses outside their major. Signing up for an abundance of elective courses is a lot like consuming empty calories. They fill up the schedule without contributing to healthy progress.

Ask your child to develop a plan that includes an ultimate timeline for graduation and the steps she will take to reach that goal. Students may not be able to identify what their major will be during the first year or two of college, but they should have a sense of when they will make that decision and how long they will take to graduate.

It matters to you if your student is not making progress toward a degree. Students who are attending classes only part-time may not qualify for medical coverage under your health insurance plan. Extra years of school add more than extra tuition; there are also additional student fees, room and board, and ultimately a delayed entry into the workforce. As soon as your student falls behind by a class or two, you should discuss how those credits can be made up, or whether a four-year plan is still logical. Most colleges and universities will accept at least a few transfer credits, so students can take summer classes at a community college or a university near home during the summer. Make sure, though, that your child checks with his adviser before taking transfer courses to be certain the credits will count and fulfill requirements. If your student is not clearly making progress toward graduation, you might decide the sensible option is for him to take a year off, work, and develop a more focused academic plan.

Many students struggle with the conflicting demands of working enough hours to afford college and studying enough hours to do well in their classes. When financial issues are overwhelming, it is hard for a student to balance study time with part-time or full-time work. The decision ends up being a matter of personal and family choice, but in the long run, students might be financially better off taking more low-interest student loans and finishing college in four or five years, rather than extending college an extra year or two in order to work more hours. The additional interest costs on college loans can be offset by the wages a graduate earns, and earlier entry into the professional world pays off in moving the college graduate beyond an entry-level position at a younger age.

WHEN YOUR STUDENT GOES BEYOND YOU

The day will come when you ask your child about school and find yourself bewildered by the response. "I am so psyched! I've been in the library all day, reading about fenestration of the fritillaries. This stuff is so cool!"

When you express confusion, your child will say, with a hint of condescension, "Fritillaries, Dad. You know, butterflies. How can I explain this so you can understand? I guess in the simplest terms, I'm doing a paper about the angle of that feathery stuff on a butterfly's wings. Never mind. It won't make any sense to you."

It's like junior high math all over again, except this time your child doesn't expect you to help. She knows she has exceeded your knowledge base, at least on one topic. This is the reward you get for supporting her all these years and for sending her to college—now she can talk down to you.

If you can show enthusiasm in your child's academic interest, you are contributing to her education. It means a lot to a student when a parent asks for more information and shares the excitement of new knowledge. There is no doubt that it can be challenging to show interest in the sentence structure of the Russian language or the characteristics of geriatric bone density. Your admiration for your student's knowledge, though, can spur her to learn more; in addition, as your child explains the subject to you, she becomes better able to talk about it to others.

Ask questions about what she is telling you, find out why she likes the subject so much, and encourage her to recommend simple books or articles about the subject for you to read. Look up the topic on the Internet. Eventually, she will achieve balance again between all the varied interests in her life, and soon enough, she will come to you for advice on what size lightbulb she needs for her desk lamp. Your status as her personal adviser on all things practical will return, and she'll appreciate *your* wisdom once again.

Progress Toward a Degree

Each of the four years of college has its own goals and milestones.

Freshman Year

During the first year at most colleges, students are exploring a liberal education. They should be taking a variety of courses representing different subjects and different learning methods. Classes that include a focus on communications skills—writing, speaking, and presentation—will provide a good foundation for other college courses and for future jobs. Ideally, by the end of the year, students will have discovered a few topics that excite them, and they will have at least a quarter of their basic education requirements completed. They should talk at least once with a career adviser to begin the process of identifying their own working styles, job-related values, and potential career paths.

Sophomore Year

The second year continues the exploration phase as students work on more of their general education coursework. The subjects that initially intrigued them are explored more thoroughly as students sign up for increasingly challenging courses. As they consider areas of study, they should be talking to counselors and career advisers about what the major means in terms of the classes they will need to take and the jobs they can pursue in that field. If career exploration courses are provided, they should take one—some career courses are specific to a major field of study; others can help identify career interests. By the end of the sophomore year, students should be prepared to declare a major.

Junior Year

Students will be taking several classes in their major this year and challenging themselves with upper-division courses. They can talk to a career adviser or the school's alumni group to find a mentor and to explore internship opportunities related to their major. By the end of the junior year, students should have a clear understanding of the career options for their major and some idea of the career direction they would like to pursue.

Senior Year

Students will be completing the coursework in their major and finishing any remaining requirements and electives. If a senior project, paper, or thesis is required, it should be planned out by the end of the first semester and completed before the end of the second semester. During the first semester, students should be working with a career adviser to explore specific employment opportunities or graduate school programs. Exams for graduate school should be taken before or during the fall semester, with grad school applications due during the fall or early winter. Students should work with their adviser to make sure all academic requirements are fulfilled and graduation forms are filled out.

QUICK TIPS FOR STUDENTS

- You will encounter some disappointments about college. Don't expect college to be a four-year vacation package.
- Remember: Your first priority in college is academics. You *do* get to have fun, but make sure that classes and homework are covered. It's sobering to realize that every course you're taking costs serious money—hundreds or even thousands of dollars. When you skip a lecture or bomb a test, you're actually wasting both time and money.
- During the first two years, take a mix of classes: large lecture, small group, and lab classes; sciences and humanities; language, writing intensive, and speech classes. If your college offers freshman seminars, take one!
- Talk to professors.
- When you're confused, when you have a problem, when you don't know what you're supposed to do next, *ask for advice*.
- Career planning begins in the first year of college. If you have

a major picked out, talk at least once to a career adviser about your long-term plans. If you do not have a major selected, or if you decide you might want to change majors, ask for help in identifying how your interests, work style, and personality might help clarify some potential jobs.

CHAPTER 5

How Can One Book Be Worth $92?

Finances Are a Family Affair

Finances are the intersection between family and student, home and college. Love and lifetime history will keep you connected, even when you don't see one another every day, but money ensures that you must talk.

No matter how mature and independent your child is by any other measure, financially he or she still is considered your legal dependent. About half of all students receive some form of financial aid,[3] and the way federal financial aid requirements are set up, parents' income is factored into the package.[4] If your child is receiving any financial assistance, it simply is not possible to draw a clear line between your finances and his as long as he is in school.

Students seem to deal best with money issues when they have a good sense of their family's financial situation. There may be details about your income and expenses that you will choose not to share with your child, but the more information you provide about college expenses and payments, the better he or she will understand the true value of an education and appreciate the contribution you are making.

Unfortunately, it's hard to discuss money dispassionately.

When Alan learned that he would be passing through his

son's college town on a job-related trip, he arranged his schedule so that he and his business partner could have dinner with his son. The two men picked Joe up from his apartment and went to one of the best restaurants in town. The dinner was excellent, and the conversation was even better. Joe was obviously excited about his classes and his friends. He talked easily with both men about his own dreams for a business career. Alan had never felt quite as proud of his son as he did that evening. Joe seemed so mature, pleasant, and confident—everything his father could have wanted.

After they finished their dinner and were looking at the dessert menu, Alan remembered the financial aid forms in his briefcase, and he mentioned that he would need a copy of Joe's tax statement and tuition receipts from the past year. "We've got to get those forms filled out for your student loans for next year. The good news is, you'll be a senior next year, and this is the last time we have to do this!"

As he spoke, Alan could see his son revert to the sullen and defiant kid he had been at sixteen. Joe slumped in his chair, checked his watch, and complained that he had to get back to his apartment. Embarrassed that his business partner was witnessing this unpleasant transformation in his son, Alan tried to change the subject and suggested that they have some dessert before leaving. That only seemed to add to Joe's irritation. "I've got a huge paper and an exam to study for. You have no idea how much work my classes are this semester!"

The mere mention of money is a reminder to students that they are still dependent on their parents. Everything that they are accomplishing at college, every vision they have for their future depends on the continuing goodwill and support of their family. While they appreciate your help and assistance, discussions of finance can bring back in a moment all the unwanted feelings of being a helpless child.

Sometimes parents don't even recognize when they're playing the "money card." When your daughter calls to ask for extra funds so that she can go with her friends to Acapulco for spring break, you might have to tell her that you set aside only enough money for her airline ticket home. "I really can't afford the extra money for you to go to Mexico for a week. I'm sorry."

This seems like a simple statement of fact to you, but it's a message of control to your daughter; she's not allowed to make her own decisions because you are in charge of all the money.

MONEY MATTERS

I've never met a student who didn't face a financial crisis during his or her college years. Even those from the wealthiest families run out of cash at some point, and all students dread asking their parents for yet another handout. Whether they overspent because of an emergency, poor planning, or an unanticipated once-in-a-lifetime opportunity, they balk at having to explain to their parents what happened and ask for more money. Between classes, in the study lounge, and anywhere students gather, we hear them comparing and worrying about their debts and expenses. Too often, though, a student's focus is on short-term finances rather than the big picture. They panic about getting through the next week or month, although what they *should* be thinking about is how the expenses they are piling up now will affect them throughout the rest of the year and even beyond graduation.

For first-year students, the problems are sadly predictable. Students begin college with a sum in their checking account—in many cases, more ready cash than they've ever had in their lives. Each day presents another chance to meet new people and do new things, but almost every opportunity involves money. Ordering a late-night pizza is hardly worth thinking about, it's just $12, split among a few roommates. An intriguing new friend recommends a must-have CD, and another $15 is gone. Everyone on the hall is going to Six Flags on the weekend, the study group for Spanish class meets at a Mexican restaurant for lunch every Tuesday, and the bookstore is having a great sale on sweatshirts. By November, the checking account is scraping bottom, and the credit card bill is out of control.

Most parents believe it is their role, not the college's, to teach their children about financial management. Even though they may expect the college to provide guidance and education about other nonacademic topics, such as sex, health, and career preparation, parents say that they will take the lead on finances. Because every family's situation is different, it really *is* the family's responsibility to make certain that their student has a realistic understanding of their circumstances and a basic level of knowledge about money, savings, and indebtedness.

Jackie's father asked her to jot down daily spending records for the first month of her freshman year as a way of helping him understand what her college expenses would be. "So far, we can only guess how much things will cost, and we might need to make some adjustments." For that first month only, he said, he would ask her to let him know each week how much she had spent for personal and entertainment expenses. "But please be careful. I'm hoping we've got enough in the savings account to cover the whole year."

By maintaining a daily record the first month of school, Jackie learned how quickly the dollars could disappear. After the first week, she had spent fully half of her September budget. When she called her father at the end of that week, she explained that she and her roommate had decided to buy matching lamps, quilts, and a rug for the dorm room. She knew when she bought the accessories that her budget would be out of balance, but she had a plan to get back on track. She could begin to make up the deficit by buying juice and snacks from the grocery store to stock her mini-fridge, rather than using the vending machines downstairs every day. Instead of going out for dinner on Sunday evening, she and her roommate agreed to fix soup and sandwiches in their room. At the end of the first month, she reported that she was still behind on her budget, but she assured her father she could be back on track within a couple of weeks. He didn't ask again for a report, but at the end of October, she told him that her finances were right where they had planned.

Each year in college presents its own financial challenges. Freshmen face hard lessons in managing checking accounts, debit cards, and credit cards. A year or two later, students move into an apartment and find themselves in a financial tailspin. As soon as they settle in, they realize they need to buy a broom and dust pan, trash bags, special connectors to hook up the TV, and toilet paper. Rent has to be paid on the first of the month, and it won't matter to the landlord if they haven't had time to get to the bank to deposit a check or transfer funds. The plan to save money by fixing meals at home falls apart when the scent of breakfast sausage wafts in from the fast-food restaurant down the block. Missing the bus to campus means hopping in the car, filling up the gas tank, and then paying an extra $5 to park for the day.

Budgets fall apart during the junior year when an unpaid internship, which will be perfect on a post-graduation résumé, causes the student to quit her part-time job in the library. A three-week, three-credit study-abroad program might cost the same as a January term class on campus, but the rent still has to be paid on that empty apartment back home while the student is using a credit card to pay for a hotel room in London.

Senior year doesn't offer any breaks. Students who are preparing for graduate school have application and testing fees and maybe a cross-country flight to interview for a fellowship. Job seekers are taking time off work and spending transportation money for job shadowing and interviews. And they must show up in a decent suit and "grown-up shoes," not sneakers or Doc Martens. This is also the time when students begin to recognize what their post-college debts will be and how those will affect their future lifestyle.

Parents and their children often have very different expectations about finances, and they most often confront the differences during school vacations. When Julie came home for semester break, her parents assumed she would replenish her bank account by picking up some shifts at the restaurant where she had worked in high school. Julie, however, thought her parents would continue giving her a weekly allowance during the break period. She was looking forward to three whole weeks of catching up on sleep, visiting with her high school friends, and making up an incomplete from her history class. She hadn't even considered calling her former boss to see if she could work a few shifts.

"Julie, it's not just that your father and I expect you to work," her mother pointed out. "Your financial aid package is based on your contributing some money toward your expenses. You can work during your breaks, or you can get a job on campus, but you need to be earning some income."

THE PAYOFF FOR PART-TIME JOBS

Parents know that college is demanding, and they don't want their student to take on more than he or she can handle. "How many hours of work are too much?" parents ask themselves. "College is so expensive, and we can't pay the full bill ourselves—should she take fewer classes each semester, work more hours, and take longer to graduate? Will we save money in the long run if she takes out fewer loans and goes to school an extra year?"

Balancing academics with employment is a challenge, and parents need to emphasize that school is the priority. Students who work more than twenty hours a week tend to see themselves as employees first and students second. When exams or major projects come up, students have a hard time reducing their work hours if it means a smaller paycheck at the end of the week.

For most freshmen, even fifteen hours of work each week can be excessive. During the first semester, a student's emphasis should be on adjustment and self-management. If students need to work that first semester, they are better off taking a position that allows flexibility and does not require learning new job skills. And they need to consider how work will fit into the academic schedule: If an exam is pending, what are the chances they can find someone to trade shifts with? How will the boss feel if they can't come in for a day or two because they have a big paper to write?

Parents and students alike tend to weigh the differences between on- and off-campus jobs by their pay rates, but jobs on campus have benefits beyond wages. Depending on the college, campus jobs might provide practical experience related to a student's major. Lab assistant or research assistant positions within a department provide an in-depth view of the field. Some schools allow upperclassmen to work as teaching assistants, grading papers or leading discussion groups under the supervision of a faculty member. A job that ties in with an academic major benefits students not only by teaching them more about the field, but also by connecting them closely with a professor. Those faculty recommendations make all the difference when the time comes to fill out internship, graduate school, or professional job applications.

Campus jobs allow students to work side by side with staff and faculty who can provide valuable guidance and advice on the school and its systems. When Rolf received an overdue library notice on a book he had returned, his work-study supervisor gave him explicit instructions. "Call Bob Givens in the Library Circulation Department, and tell him that you put the book in the return slot on Thursday morning before the library opened. Maybe they sent out those notices before they checked in the books in the drop box. Bob will look it up for you."

Commuter students, especially, benefit from on-campus jobs. The support systems and social opportunities that come with working on campus provide a sense of belonging and a circle of friends. Having a desk or a work space provides a campus "home" for commuters. "I have a place to drop my books between classes, and the people I work with let me use the microwave and refrigerator, even on days when I'm not working," Tina says.

BASIC TOOLS FOR MONEY MANAGEMENT

You may believe that you have communicated clearly about finances, but your student might not agree. Every time I ask a roomful of parents "How many of you have talked to your student about finances and credit cards?" about 90 percent of them raise their hands. However, when I ask students "Have your parents talked to you about finances and credit cards?" only about one-third say yes.

As Keesha explained, "I'm sure they told me to watch my expenses and not to sign up for any credit cards, but that's not the same as *talking* about finances. They never told me what problems I might have, or why I shouldn't get a credit card. I mean, *they* have credit cards. Everyone does. I wish they had told me how easy it is to let spending get out of control and how expensive it can be when you overdraw your checking account or when you don't pay your credit card bill on time."

Students have a head start on college success if they know how to manage and balance a checking account, understand family expectations about who pays for which expenses, and know how their parents feel about credit and debit cards well before they leave home. Your child already has a sense of how you manage your money—in fact, one of the best predictors of a student's financial problems is her parents' level of debt. Money management, however, is not a topic that can be learned solely by observation or by lectures. Students need practice and skill building. Discussions between parents and their child before school starts provide a foundation, but they won't necessarily forestall all problems.

As a sophomore, Phil carefully rationalized the need for multiple credit cards: "I had a Discover card for my computer. It was an expensive computer, so I pretty much maxed out that account. I had a Visa for groceries. I made sure I bought all my clothes on my Gap card so I could keep my clothing budget separate from everything else. Then I had a MasterCard for emergencies—my car was having a lot of problems, so that balance was a lot higher than I wanted it to be. And I had a Target card because, you know, you have to buy soap and cleaning supplies and just . . . stuff."

After a year of juggling five separate accounts, Phil caught on that this was not what his parents meant when they told him about financial management.

Students need some guidance in reviewing and reconciling a monthly checking account statement, and they need to understand the penalties for overdrafts. They need a plan for keeping track of debit card payments. Before they apply for their first credit card, they should know about the fine print on applications and the implications of annual fees and temporarily reduced interest rates. Some parents start their child with a checking account and credit card in high school or during the first semester of college, then they monitor the accounts. By co-signing for a credit card with a low limit—$300 or $500—parents have some assurance that their student won't go seriously into debt, and they use the monthly bills to discuss purchasing decisions and the consequences of late payments. A debit card can provide some of the convenience of credit cards without the risk of running up interest charges, as long as the card prevents withdrawing more than is in the account. When students get to college, many parents co-sign for a credit card or debit card and agree to pay only for expenses the student clears with them in advance.

Student loans make up the biggest debt that college students face after graduation, but credit cards create the greatest financial problems. By all indications, college students can get credit cards more easily than can young adults who have jobs. Every fall, tables appear on campus or in nearby shopping malls, offering free T-shirts, a crisp $5 bill, coupons for fast food, or a candy bar in exchange for filling out a credit card application. Applicants don't need to prove they have an income; they can simply indicate that they are enrolled in college. They rarely take time to read the fine print, and most vow they will cut up the card when it arrives. "No way do I need another credit card, but check out this T-shirt! The color's great, and it means I can go another day without doing laundry."

The self-promise to cut up the new card doesn't always work out as planned. In some cases, by signing up for a card, students have agreed to charges they did not foresee; shortly after the card arrives, they receive a bill listing a $25 enrollment charge or a $50 annual fee. Too often, a student realizes she has maxed out her first, parent-approved credit card, but the new one arrives just in time to pay for an ink cartridge for her printer. If the bills from that original card are being sent home, this new one means the student can buy what she wants without her parents' seeing the statement and asking any questions.

As the debts mount, the student figures she's doing well to keep up with the minimum monthly payments, but the low introductory interest rate of 8 percent turns out to be only temporary. For $2,000 in credit card debt at 17.9 percent interest, the interest payment alone will cost $29 a month. Paying $35 a month, it will take more than ten years to erase the debt.[5] That's with no new charges. To clear the account in one year, payments will be more than $180 per month. If one payment is missed, in addition to late payment penalties, the interest rate is likely to jump another 6 percent.

A survey conducted in 2000 by Nellie Mae, a student-loan provider, indicated that more than three-fourths of all students have credit cards and that the average student has three. The typical outstanding debt among college students was $2,748, up from $1,879 only two years earlier.[6]

Credit cards are a part of our national economy, and they are a convenience when used with care. Most parents say they want their child to have a credit card for emergencies, and they recognize that Internet commerce requires payment with a credit card. Parents have pointed out that when their child studies abroad, a credit card is the best way to manage expenses. They brag that by charging their child's tuition and room and board payments, they can accumulate enough frequent flyer miles to trade for their student's trip home for the holidays. Meanwhile, about 10 percent of students nationally have more than $7,000 in credit card debt, and it will take them years to repay what they owe.[7]

Signs of Trouble

The following are common signs of credit card mismanage-ment:[8]

- Making only minimum payments on the credit card bill for three or more consecutive months
- Missing payments
- Using credit cards for cash advances
- Consistently keeping a balance on the account that is near or at the card's maximum limit allowed
- Applying for multiple credit cards

EMPHASIZE FINANCIAL SKILLS

You urge your student to be responsible about finances and to be cautious about his expenditures. Too often, however, students make choices they believe will save money, but that have un-anticipated consequences.

Midway through his sophomore year, James tallied up his checking account and realized he was not going to have enough money to make it through the rest of the year. He looked at ways to reduce his expenses and saw that the biggest check he wrote every week was for groceries. If he could reduce that amount, he could save a few hundred dollars by the end of the year.

Many students look at food as the most obvious way to cut expenses. Certainly, there are ways to reduce the grocery bill, but meals are not the best choice when it comes to saving money. A steady diet of ramen noodles, while cheap, is not nutritious, and it will end up costing them in energy and health. Late-night snacks can't be cut out of the routine, but groceries are still a good investment. Encourage your student to stick with a good diet and find other ways to trim expenses.

Few teenagers have a realistic concept of living expenses until they pay the bills themselves. They receive an allowance or income from a job, and they know what they can buy with those dollars. They probably don't, however, understand life's basic costs—the grocery bill, the house mortgage, the car payments, the various insurance costs. They may know those expenses exist, but they don't have a grasp of how it all adds up. They understand best the expenses that they, themselves, have directly affected in the past: The phone bill, in their experience, is all about long-distance charges; that monthly connection fee has never been their issue. They know the exact cost of a burger and fries; the grocery bill is a foreign concept.

Students need to know the overall cost of their college education, but such a big sum, stretching over four years, might seem incomprehensible at first. If you break down the total into monthly and annual expenses, your student can see more clearly the financial impact of the decisions she is making. You will do your whole family a favor by working through a budget with your child each year. Defining your student's role in the finances will empower him by acknowledging the importance of working, saving, and making plans to repay college loans. A solid understanding of the finances before school starts will give your student the necessary background to make good decisions when there are choices to be made.

You can help your child develop financial skills, but it takes time, patience, and perseverance to work through the steps.

- *Encourage—and teach—your child to keep financial records.* You will need the records for tax purposes, and there will be times when your student will need proof of a payment or a receipt for some item. A week after classes begin, if he decides his advanced calculus class is too difficult and he wants to switch to an introductory math class, he will be able to return his calculus textbook only if he can find the receipt. Make sure your

child knows that he must keep bank statements, tuition statements, receipts and warranties for all major purchases, credit
card agreements, scholarship records, and loan agreements.

- *Organize a file for financial records.* During the first year of
  school, a single folder for finances in the college file box might
  be sufficient. Freshmen can file all major financial receipts and
  records together. As a general rule of thumb, if a folder
  becomes too bulky to manage easily, it should be arranged
  into two or more folders. When students move to an apartment, or if you agree that more organization is needed, a separate file box just for financial records will be helpful. Let your
  student decide if it makes more sense to organize records by
  month—putting all receipts and statements for a month into
  one envelope or folder—or by category, such as academic
  expenses, room and board, communications, transportation.
  Encourage him or her to get into the habit of filing receipts
  and statements faithfully.
- *Be sure your student knows what records are required for tax purposes
  and for student loan or scholarship applications.* Even if you are
  paying most of the bills, your student will probably receive the
  statements and receipts. Discuss how you will communicate
  about those documents. If you need them for tax purposes,
  how and when will you get them?

BUDGETING: A BALANCING ACT

In the long run, students learn best through experience—their
own and the experiences of their brothers, sisters, and friends.
"My older sister got into serious trouble with credit cards, and
she had to quit school and get a job so she could pay them off. I
am *never* going to let that happen!"

Financial management is critical to becoming a responsible
adult. Your role is not to make your child's financial decisions but
to give him or her the foundation for making smart choices. Stu-

dents *do* have expenses for entertainment, health and wellness, snacks, haircuts, the occasional new pair of socks, and emergencies. Your student can adjust funds between categories as the semester goes by—"I can save money by having my roommate cut my hair, and then I can spend my haircut money on CDs!" Making a realistic budget together, though, is the first step to making it through the year without racking up unexpected debt.

How to Plan a College Budget

1. Figure out your education resources. You can start out with the school's cost of attendance—the sum of tuition, fees, and living expenses estimated by the college. It's as good a guess as any. But bear in mind that this figure is just what the college tells you a year of college will cost; no one spends exactly the predicted amount.

2. Next, fill in the numbers that show which resources these anticipated funds will come from—the grants, scholarships, loans, and cash contributions that the school, the government, you, and your student will each be contributing to your student's education.

3. Then figure out your college budget expenses. Go through the various expense categories, filling in the cost-certain numbers and estimating the rest. Remember that the totals should reflect costs for all sessions, including the summer session.

4. Finally, figure out how much from each educational resource (parents; students; grants, loans, and scholarships) will be used for each expense category. Remind your student that the expense totals cannot exceed the resource totals. Your student will begin to see that his decisions can allow flexibility in some of the numbers, and you will have an opportunity to assess your student's strengths and weaknesses in budget planning.

Education Resources

What is your college's estimated yearly cost of attendance?

$_____

Fill in the following to determine how you will fund that cost.

Grants $_____

Scholarships $_____

Parent Contribution $_____

   Parent loan $_____

   Parents' savings $_____

   Parents' monthly contribution from income $_____

Student Contribution $_____

   Student loan $_____

   Student's savings $_____

   Student's monthly contribution from income $_____

College Budget

	EXPENSES	RESOURCES		
	Yearly Total	Parents	Student	Grants/Loans/ Scholarships
EDUCATION EXPENSES				
Fixed Costs				
Tuition	$_____	$_____	$_____	$_____
Fees	$_____	$_____	$_____	$_____

Discussion point: Is there anything that could affect these costs? Some schools provide "tuition caps" for students who take a certain number of credits, for example, a per-credit tuition rate for up to 12 credits and a flat fee for 13 or more credits.

EXPENSES	RESOURCES		
Yearly Total	Parents	Student	Grants/Loans/ Scholarships

EDUCATION EXPENSES (continued)

Estimated Costs

Books	$____	$____	$____	$____
Supplies	$____	$____	$____	$____

Discussion point: What factors might either raise or lower these expenses? It is cheaper to buy used books, resell books at the end of the semester, and stock up on supplies during the summer to take advantage of back-to-school sales. Does the college require a laptop computer? Is there special software that your curriculum will require?

ROOM/HOUSING

Fixed Costs

Room contract or rent	$____	$____	$____	$____
Damage deposit	$____	$____	$____	$____
Utilities (basic service)	$____	$____	$____	$____
Phone, computer, TV (basic service)	$____	$____	$____	$____

Discussion point: Is there anything that could affect these costs? Will the student be renting a dorm refrigerator or loft for the bed? Is broadband worth the expense? Is cable TV necessary in this community? Would subscribing to movie channels reduce the likelihood of renting videos, or would it just be another expense?

Estimated Costs

Room or apartment decorating	$____	$____	$____	$____

EXPENSES	RESOURCES		
Yearly Total	Parents	Student	Grants/Loans/ Scholarships

ROOM/HOUSING (continued)

Utilities (usage charges) $____	$____	$____	$____
Phone, computer, TV (usage charges)$____	$____	$____	$____

Discussion point: What factors might either raise or lower these expenses? Could a telephone calling card reduce long-distance charges? Will a cell phone raise or lower these expenses?

FOOD

Fixed Costs

Meal plan or groceries $____	$____	$____	$____

Discussion point: Is there anything that could affect these costs? Can meal plans be changed mid-semester if the student is not using all his meals?

Estimated Costs

Meals not covered by meal plan $____	$____	$____	$____
Snacks not covered by meal plan $____	$____	$____	$____

Discussion point: What factors might either raise or lower these expenses? If the student misses meals covered by the meal plan, who will pay for dining out?

PERSONAL EXPENSES

Estimated Costs

Clothing $____	$____	$____	$____

	EXPENSES	RESOURCES		
	Yearly Total	Parents	Student	Grants/Loans/ Scholarships

PERSONAL EXPENSES (continued)

Laundry	$____	$____	$____	$____
Toiletries	$____	$____	$____	$____
Household (cleaning items)	$____	$____	$____	$____
Haircuts and personal expenses	$____	$____	$____	$____

Discussion point: What factors might either raise or lower these expenses? Are haircuts cheaper at home than on campus?

HEALTH AND WELLNESS

Fixed Costs

Health insurance	$____	$____	$____	$____
Prescriptions, medications	$____	$____	$____	$____
Medical appointments (doctor, dentist, optometrist, etc.)	$____	$____	$____	$____

Discussion point: Is there anything that could affect these costs?

Estimated Costs

Medical appointments	$____	$____	$____	$____
Prescriptions, medications	$____	$____	$____	$____
Unscheduled medical costs	$____	$____	$____	$____
Recreation or health club fees	$____	$____	$____	$____

Discussion point: What factors might either raise or lower these expenses? If there are co-payments, who will pay? Will parents provide extra funds if the student needs medication not covered by insurance? If parents receive a bill for services, what are the expectations about explanations?

	EXPENSES	RESOURCES		
	Yearly Total	Parents	Student	Grants/Loans/ Scholarships

TRANSPORTATION

Fixed Costs

	EXPENSES	RESOURCES		
Bus fare or pass	$____	$____	$____	$____
Transportation costs to and from school (airfare, cab, etc.)	$____	$____	$____	$____
Car payments, if applicable	$____	$____	$____	$____
Scheduled car maintenance	$____	$____	$____	$____
Insurance, if applicable	$____	$____	$____	$____
Parking, if applicable	$____	$____	$____	$____

Discussion point: Is there anything that could affect these costs? For example, how will parking tickets be handled? What if the student wants to come home for the weekend, and the budget does not allow for the additional transportation costs?

Estimated Costs

	EXPENSES	RESOURCES		
Bus fares	$____	$____	$____	$____
Gas	$____	$____	$____	$____
Parking, noncontract	$____	$____	$____	$____
Repairs	$____	$____	$____	$____

Discussion point: What factors might either raise or lower these expenses?

EXPENSES	RESOURCES		
Yearly Total	Parents	Student	Grants/Loans/ Scholarships

ENTERTAINMENT

Fixed Costs

Athletic season tickets $____	$____	$____	$____
Concert season tickets $____	$____	$____	$____
Other $____	$____	$____	$____

Discussion point: What factors might either raise or lower these expenses?

Estimated Costs

Movies, videos, concerts $____	$____	$____	$____
Books, CDs, magazines $____	$____	$____	$____
Dating, socializing $____	$____	$____	$____

Discussion point: What factors might either raise or lower these expenses? What if a great concert comes to town, but its cost is beyond the entertainment budget? What if the team qualifies for a postseason tournament or game?

INTEREST PAYMENTS

Fixed Costs

Educational loans (some are due while the student is still in school) $____	$____	$____	$____

Discussion point: Is there anything that could affect these costs? What if financial issues require an emergency loan?

EXPENSES	RESOURCES		
Yearly Total	Parents	Student	Grants/Loans/ Scholarships

INTEREST PAYMENT (continued)

Estimated Costs

Credit card interest $____	$____	$____	$____

Discussion point: What factors might either raise or lower these expenses? How would a late payment affect the cost, and who will pay any penalty charges?

OTHER

Fixed Costs

Savings $____	$____	$____	$____

Discussion point: It is important to start setting aside funds each year for future expenses. What factors might either raise or lower these amounts?

Estimated Costs

Other anticipated expenses $____	$____	$____	$____
Miscellaneous unanticipated expenses, including emergencies $____	$____	$____	$____

Discussion point: What factors might either raise or lower these expenses? What if electronics need repair? Do you see a difference between computer repair or replacement and repair or replacement of a TV or CD player?

Cell Phone, Calling Plan, or Phone Card?

Wading through the many options for phone service can be confusing. Does your student need a cellular phone, or is that an extra expense the family can avoid? What kind of calling plan makes the most sense? Is it possible to find one plan that can be used for all calls? Students who live in an apartment might use their phone jack as a computer hookup, which means the phone is unavailable whenever the Internet is in use. Is a second phone line the logical solution?

Calling Plans

The college or university your student is attending will have information on whether residence hall students have a choice of long-distance calling plans. Students living in an off-campus apartment will probably need to choose among several different alternatives.

Where there are options, talk with your student about choices and calling patterns. Is there a plan that will provide less-expensive rates during off-peak hours? If so, are the off-peak hours going to fit a schedule that will work for your child? If your student attends college in Oregon but you (and his friends) are on the East Coast, he will not have much use for cheap rates that kick in after 11 P.M. Back home, it will be 2 A.M., and you will wake up in a panic when the phone rings.

If your student has a choice of long-distance providers, ask if she will be able to change plans when calling patterns become clear. Toward the end of the first semester, your child can review the phone bills to determine when most calls are made, and she can decide if another plan might be more affordable.

Calling Cards and Dial-Around Plans

Calling cards offer flexibility, since they can be used from any phone. Dial-around plans (the 10-10 numbers you use from your own phone) offer some of the least expensive per-minute charges. Both have their benefits and drawbacks.

Calling cards can be inexpensive, but your student needs to be alert to the fine print. Watch for activation fees and surcharges, and take note of limitations and expiration dates. Some cards can be used only for calls outside one's own state. Some allow international calling, and some do not. And find out what happens if calls exceed the minutes provided by the card.

Dial-around plans are useful only from the user's own telephone, unless they are connected to a credit card or calling card. Students probably won't be able to use them from a friend's phone or a pay phone. The per-minute rate may be inexpensive, but a connection charge will negate any bargains. If your student makes a call and connects to an answering machine, he might leave only a thirty-second message but be charged for a ten-minute phone call.

A phone card can be useful for emergencies, and dial-around plans provide the best bargains when your student knows someone will answer the phone. You might consider both as part of a comprehensive telephone plan.

Cell Phone

Many parents regard cell phones as a form of insurance. In an emergency, they want their child to be able to place a call, no matter where she is. But cell phones can also create their own emergencies. A lost or stolen phone means quick calls to cancel service. Extra costs from using minutes over the plan limits or unexpected roaming charges can break a student's budget.

If you decide on a cell phone, talk to your student about the plan limits; talk about who will pay for the basic phone plan and who will pay for long-distance charges and any extra fees for roaming or out-of-plan calls. The cell phone that a student used in high school may not be the best option in the college community. Unless all long-distance charges are included in the plan, be sure to get a phone number in the area code where the phone will be used most. With many cellular services, including long-distance minutes in the plan means a more expensive monthly fee, but it may be more convenient to have all expenses on one bill. In some cases, access is not available to or from certain service areas.

Phone Rates for International Calls

When students go abroad for international study or for recreational travel, an international calling plan will save you both money and worry. Contact your long-distance provider to ask about rates for calls placed to or from the country where your child will be. By paying a small monthly service fee on your home phone bill, you can usually get rates that are much less expensive for collect calls, comparable to interstate long-distance phone rates.

QUICK TIPS FOR STUDENTS

- As with other issues that fall under the heading "Life Is Unfair," none of your friends is in the same financial situation as you are. Don't try to match your spending to theirs. Don't feel guilty for what you have or shamed by what you don't have, and don't ever be afraid to say "I can't afford that." Everyone knows that college students never have enough money to buy everything they want.

- Your finances are tied to your parents'. If you are receiving college loans, your parents' income is figured into the formula until you're twenty-four. That means some of the choices you make will affect their financial situation. Talk to your parents about any decisions that will have an impact on them.

- Keep your receipts, file them in an accordion file or a file cabinet, and make sure your parents get copies of the statements they need for their income tax.

- Beware the small print on credit and debit card applications—you may be agreeing to an annual fee, an enrollment fee, or overdraft penalties. Make sure you understand the terms and conditions for any credit card you get. Remember: If you don't pay your entire bill this month, you will pay interest next month. And the company will collect its interest payment from your check before it subtracts anything from the amount you owe.

- Watch everything for deadlines and payment dates. Filling out a scholarship application a day after the deadline is a waste of time—you're not going to get the scholarship. Pay credit card bills as soon as you receive them. Payment dates are based on when your check arrives at the processing center, not when you mail the check, and late payments mean penalty charges. On credit cards, a late payment might also mean a big increase in the interest rate you are charged.

- One more caution regarding credit cards: That free T-shirt, pen, or candy bar that you can receive by filling out a credit card application is not really free! The credit card company is betting that you will pay for that giveaway one way or another.

CHAPTER 6

Sex, Drugs, and Drinking Games

The Social Scene

When newly admitted students talk about the one best thing college will offer, they say "freedom" or "independence." The issues that parents worry most about, though, the ones they can hardly bear to acknowledge, are the choices that independence will mean for their child in three areas: sex, drugs, and alcohol. The wrong decisions in any of these three areas have the potential of changing—even ruining—a young person's life.

As a parent, you have probably been reciting the lectures for years: Don't drink; say no to drugs; sex can lead to pregnancy and disease. Now, when you mention these topics, your child's eyes glaze over, and you get the look that says "I know what you're going to say, and I don't need to hear it again."

They're right—they do know what you're going to say. When it comes to sex, drugs, and alcohol, your children know how you feel. Nevertheless, you *will* worry, and it doesn't hurt to repeat your values from time to time, with positive and supportive messages rather than lectures. In the long run, the best parents can do is offer the background guidance and promote the moral strength their child needs in order to make a *choice* each time the opportunity comes up. We often forget that sex, drugs, and alcohol are not one-time decisions. When your first-year student leaves for college, he may pledge not to drink, but if his roommate offers to share a bottle of whiskey some Saturday evening, he may decide to take a shot. That does not mean he has become a drinker. The next time he's offered a drink, he can still say no. Unless your student loses the ability to make that choice, your advice will continue to have an impact.

SUBSTANCE ABUSE—A COLLEGE EPIDEMIC OR JUST KIDS BEING KIDS?

Everyone says it: "College students drink." They know that drugs are available on campus. You've read the news articles, and you've seen *Animal House*. Watch any college football game on TV on a Saturday afternoon in the fall, and you can pick out the tipsy fans in the crowd. So what are the odds that your child will get through college without drinking or using drugs? After all, by the time kids finish high school, nearly 80 percent admit that they have tried alcohol, and more than 50 percent of high school seniors have used drugs.[9]

"Just don't be stupid about it," parents say. To some extent, parents are simply relieved that it's out of their hands. "There's nothing I can do. At least while he's living on campus, he won't be drinking and driving. He can walk to the parties."

But everyone also knows that college students die every year in accidents related to alcohol and drugs. Driving drunk or riding with a drunk driver is the greatest risk among college students, but a student also might trip and fall down a flight of stairs when he's walking home from a party.

How can you tell if your child is at risk? There seem to be three factors that serve as strong predictors to a student's drinking or drug use:

- The student's alcohol or drug history during high school.
- The parents' use of, and attitude toward, alcohol or drugs.
- The culture of the particular college.

Student's Alcohol or Drug History During High School

The student who drank excessively in high school is not likely to quit when he goes to college. That's not to say your child is hopeless if he partied too much on prom night or smoked a joint that one time after graduation. He might have learned a good lesson when he woke up sick the next morning or had to face angry friends or family. A few slipups don't mean he has a major problem.

On the other hand, if your child equates drinking with having a good time, he will continue to drink in college. If your child got drunk on a regular basis in high school, he may have a serious problem. And if he experimented frequently with drugs in high school, there's a very good chance he will use drugs in college.

Unfortunately, many students already have substance abuse problems by the time they arrive at college. The college population represents every possible level of drinking and drug use, from total abstinence to addiction. Some 10 percent of the college population will become bona fide alcoholics, for all the same reasons that adults become alcoholics. Another 19 percent will not drink at all.[10] Students, like their parents, vary widely in their beliefs and behaviors regarding drinking and drugs.

Parents' Use of, and Attitude Toward, Alcohol or Drugs

Some parents are shocked and disbelieving when they get a call saying that their child has been cited for drinking—not because he was drunk, but because anyone cares. "Of course, he was drinking. He's a college student," they say. Or they explain, "We allow him to drink at home. He knows his limits."

Even the child of nondrinkers might start drinking two weeks after college begins, though, simply because "everyone drinks." Similarly, the student who never considered drug use before college might begin to use drugs, because he comes to believe that "It's not really a big deal."

The Culture of the Particular College

Peer pressure is at work on campus. There are colleges where drinking is part of the overall atmosphere. And although there is probably some drug use at any college, the type of drugs and the extent of use varies from one college to another. Within a single university, students might be heavier drinkers in one particular residence hall, or there may be more drug use among students on one floor of a dorm. Studies have shown that student athletes generally drink more than nonathletes, and fraternity and sorority members tend to drink more than non-greeks.[11] Some colleges have a "party school" reputation. That does not mean, however, that all fraternity members drink, everyone in the poetry club is a stoner, or everyone at the university gets drunk every weekend.

What it does mean is that if "everyone is doing it," risky behavior feels much less dangerous.

IT'S ILLEGAL, SO MAKE THEM STOP!

Drinking has been called the number one problem among college students. It leads to poor grades, sexual assaults, fights, vandalism, wasted time, and wasted money. By some estimates, students spend more on beer every year than they spend on textbooks—and textbooks are expensive.

If alcohol is such a predictable problem, parents wonder, why don't colleges do something about it? Midway through the first semester, Dwayne's father called the university president, demanding, "You have to stop the drinking on campus! My son's roommate gets drunk with his friends every weekend, and my kid can't even study in his own room because of the noise. The law says you have to be twenty-one to drink, but the cops have this 'nudge-nudge, wink-wink' attitude, and you just let it continue. What has to happen before you do something about it?"

Colleges are not blindly standing by while their underage students drink. Truly, professors do not want hungover, unprepared students in their classrooms. Residence hall staff would prefer not to deal with students who are loud, drunk, or disorderly. Every campus has policies regarding underage drinking. Most colleges and universities do not, however, routinely search students' rooms, nor do they conduct random checks for alcohol or drugs. Privacy laws prevent staff members from invading students' personal space without cause; students and their parents would rightly object to searches of innocent students' rooms. Consequently, the quiet student who might have a six-pack of beer in the refrigerator, or who is smoking marijuana and blowing the smoke out the window may not be caught. It's the "noise and nuisance" behaviors that alert staff members to drinking and drugs, and those cases are confronted.

As we mentioned in chapter 3, a change in the Family Educational Rights and Privacy Act (FERPA) a few years ago makes it an option for schools to notify parents in cases of alcohol and drug violations. There is no universal standard for parent notification, though. At some schools, families will be notified if a student is merely *charged* with a violation. Others will wait until a student has gone through the judicial process and been found guilty of the charge. Some will notify after a second or third conviction, or if the student is about to face eviction from the residence hall. Still others have decided they will not notify parents without the student's knowledge and permission, except in life-threatening situations.

Anyone with $20 and an Internet connection can order a fake

identification card. If they have a creative friend, a good computer printer, and a laminating machine, students don't even have to wait the two days to get their ID through the mail. Then again, who needs identification when they know where the keg party is?

HOW WORRIED SHOULD I BE?

Parents of today's college students remember when the drinking age was lowered from twenty-one to eighteen or nineteen throughout most of the United States. Many parents remember celebrating their own eighteenth birthday by drinking legally. But in 1984, federal legislation was passed to phase the drinking limit back up to the age of twenty-one. The reasoning was that alcohol-related automobile accidents were rising, and there was evidence that eighteen-year-olds were passing alcohol along to their seventeen-, sixteen-, and fifteen-year-old high school friends.

While driving under the influence of alcohol remains a significant issue for underage drinkers, a new troublesome trend is the increase in heavy, or binge, drinking and drinking games. At both the high school and college levels, the goal is not just to drink but to get drunk as quickly and cheaply as possible.

Students believe that since they're not drinking and driving, they are safe. They're out with friends, so someone will take care of them. They ask one person to "babysit" the group to make sure no one falls asleep on his back, thinking that will protect them from vomit asphyxiation. They choose not to consider the dangers of other types of accidents—college students are injured or die every year from alcohol-induced fights, alcohol-related falls, hypothermia, and alcohol poisoning. They hear their friends joke about how drunk they got on the weekend, and they pass over the warnings about legal limits of intoxication. "You're not actually going to die from drinking beer," they figure. They know plenty of people who took a six-pack to a party and came safely home. "Maybe if you drank a couple bottles of whiskey, you'd be in trouble, but you'll get sick from beer and wine before anything really bad happens," they tell themselves.

Students don't want to hear lectures about drinking, but they pay attention when they hear statistics that they can apply to themselves. Men listen when they're told that four drinks within an hour will put a 180-pound male over the legal limit for blood alcohol content. Women will take notice when they hear that six beers within an hour could turn fatal for someone who weighs 120 pounds.

Blood Alcohol Level Estimates

BAL indicates the number of milliliters of alcohol in 100 milliliters of a person's blood.

No. of Drinks	120 lb. Woman	180 lb. Man
1	.04	.03
2	.08	.05
3	.13	.08
4	.17	.11
5	.21	.14
6	.26	.16
7	.30	.19
8	.33	.22

Binge drinking, or heavy drinking, is typically defined as four or more drinks in a single sitting for a woman or five or more drinks in a sitting for a man. This level has been targeted as dangerous because it is where negative outcomes of drinking tend to show up. Emotions, either positive or negative, are exaggerated. Judgment is impaired, and the risks increase for unplanned sex, accidents, arguments, and fights. Blackouts can occur at a BAL as low as .15 percent. At .20 BAL, nausea and vomiting are common. At .25, physical sensors may be sufficiently numb to result in asphyxiation from vomiting. Death from alcohol poisoning may occur around .30, and at .40, the brain fails to signal heartbeats and breathing.

Source: http://www.factsontap.org/yourbody/yourbody.htm

Fortunately, it is rare for a student *not* to survive a night of heavy drinking. She may suffer temporary negative consequences—a hangover, a scraped knee from stumbling into a fence, a wallet left at the bar, or an angry friend. But there also are the long-term consequences. Students who drink heavily have lower grade point averages than nondrinkers. A study by the CORE Institute indicated that students who earn A's in college average three drinks per week, while B students average five drinks per week, C students average about seven drinks per week, and D and F students average about eleven drinks per week. Students who drink heavily are five to six times more likely to miss classes and fall behind in their schoolwork.[12]

DRUGS—THE LOW-CAL HIGH

Risky behaviors extend to drug use, and students can creatively justify their use by claiming the highs are less messy (no vomiting, no empties to toss) and less fattening ("All those empty calories in beer—no, thanks!"). Marijuana is the most readily available drug on college campuses, and—as with alcohol—students often arrive as freshmen with experience in buying and using marijuana. The National Institute of Drug Abuse reports that more than a third of high school seniors report use of marijuana during the past year, and nearly half have used marijuana or hashish at least once in their life. Hard drugs, such as cocaine, heroin, and crack cocaine, are much less prevalent on college campuses. At the college level, use of marijuana tends to go in cycles, and recent years have seen a troubling increase. Colleges and universities have responded by developing zero-tolerance policies, and a student who is found with marijuana or drug paraphernalia is likely to face automatic expulsion from the residence hall.

Students generally do not want to take the risk of hard drugs, but increasingly they are willing to gamble with club drugs and prescription drugs. They think they are playing it safe using the old standbys—beer or liquor—mixed with relatively common prescriptions, such as Ritalin or Valium: "These are legal! What can it hurt to wash down a pill with a drink? You get stoned faster, and the high lasts longer." They can even get their health insurance to pay for the pills if they fake symptoms. They don't want to know they are creating potentially lethal cocktails, so they don't pay attention to the warning labels that say "Do not mix with alcohol." They choose not to worry about the memory lapses or the lingering effects a day later.

The so-called club drugs—tablets or liquids that have found their way into the party scene—pose particular problems when combined with alcohol. GHB (gamma hydroxybutyrate) and Rohypnol are showing up on college campuses across the country and are associated with date rape. These drugs are clear and odorless, nearly impossible to detect in a drink. With recipes posted on the Internet and available for bargain prices in Mexican spring break resorts, they are easy to buy or to make and despairingly effective. Victims rarely have the time or ability to recognize the symptoms of the drug, and the traces disappear from the bloodstream within twenty-four hours. By the time a victim begins to understand what happened, it is usually too late to gather evidence.

Because the purity and strength of these drugs is unknown, their danger is even greater. Mixed with alcohol, they can cause coma and death.

PREVENTION PARTNERSHIPS

Parents might feel more comfortable after hearing that the school will contact them if their child violates drug or drinking policies, but by the time a problem shows up, parent notification might not make a difference. Increasingly, colleges are hearing from parents after a serious incident: "Someone is supposed to be watching these kids. I trusted you to look out for my child. How could you let us down?"

Even at small, private colleges where staff members do their best to monitor student behavior closely, they cannot prevent every incident. At a large university where students have much more personal freedom, it is not possible for the school to monitor every student. Students must take responsibility for their own behavior, and colleges need parents' help in reinforcing that message.

Increasingly, college students are becoming assertive about their rights to a clean and quiet residence hall. In past years, students who didn't drink or use drugs were willing to accept their housemates' behavior, however annoying it may have been. They bought into the messages that most college students drink and that drugs were not a problem. Now, though, students who stumble into the residence hall after a weekend party, waking up their neighbors or throwing up in the bathrooms, are much more likely to be reported to hall staff or confronted the next day about their disruptive behavior.

If your student complains about a roommate's or neighbor's drinking or drug use, you can encourage him to talk to the residence hall adviser or hall director. You also can give your child permission to use you as an excuse if friends are pushing him to join the party. Back in junior high and high school, the standard advice was that children could say their parents would not allow them to drink or take drugs: "My mom will kill me if she finds out. And my mother knows *everything* I do. The woman is spooky." Now the message may include a college angle: "My parents would make me move home if they ever heard I was messing around. I'm having too much fun here to have to go back home!"

This is one area where you can allow your student to make up stories: "My parole officer said he'd bust me if he catches me doing that stuff again. I want to be a chef, not a prison cook."

Students tend to rationalize their drinking by claiming stress: "We work so hard that we have to play hard, too." Or they rely on the old standbys: "All college students drink." "It's a stupid law—what makes twenty-one the magic number?"

Parents can support the college's efforts to control drug use by letting students know that not all college students drink to excess. And they can call their student on the excuses: "You can have fun without drugs and alcohol." "Even if it *is* a stupid law, it's still the law, and there are penalties for breaking it." You are justified in letting your student know you will not pay tens of thousands of dollars to fund a four-year party.

On the other hand, a single drinking incident or a couple of beers at a party are not justification for pulling your student out of school. There is truth to the theory that college students are educable. They learn from their mistakes, and many eighteen-year-olds decide after one serious drinking bout that a blackout is too steep a price to pay for an evening of indulgence.

Although your expectations are important, your student is in an awkward stage between youth and maturity. These are decisions you cannot make for your child. But if you find that your child is partying more than you'd like, hang on to a ray of hope.

When students leave college and move into the real world of employment and responsibility, most of them quit their excessive drinking and drug taking. Once the peer pressure is removed, throwing up and hangovers lose their appeal.[13]

THE COLLEGE DRINKING CALENDAR

Some of the high periods of drinking and drug use in college are predictable. Although any student might decide to get wasted on any given weekend, there are times when heavy and dangerous drinking is more likely. The highest levels of drinking occur during the freshman year, and especially in the first few weeks of the freshman year.[14] First-year students are anxious about meeting new friends, and going to parties gives them the sense that they are socializing. Alcohol makes them less self-conscious. And, of course, freshmen are reveling in their newfound freedom.[15]

Sophomores generally do less serious drinking, but toward the end of the junior year and into the senior year, dangerous drinking peaks again as students celebrate their own and their friends' twenty-first birthdays.

No matter the student's academic class standing, certain times of the year are more likely to spur drinking:

- *The first two weeks of classes of every academic term.* Students are meeting new friends or celebrating reunions with returning friends. Alcohol eases social situations. Students haven't established study schedules yet, so it feels as if there's more free time. Homework assignments and deadlines are still in the distance.
- *Football games and homecoming.* Pre- and post-game parties are traditions at many football schools. Homecoming and Halloween are big party nights, and the stress of midterms is an easy excuse to use alcohol.

- *Finals*. Stress and the intensity of studying mesh with unstructured study days and exam days. Celebrating the last final is a ritual at some colleges.
- *Midwinter weekends and winter or spring celebrations*. In cold-weather climates, drinking may be the winter pastime. Campus festivals often coincide with the conclusion of midterm exams.
- *Spring break*. Escapes to warm locations bring students together from all around the country. The partying is legendary.
- *The end of the academic year*. Students plan gatherings with friends before leaving for the summer. Seniors, old enough to drink legally, are beginning the graduation festivities at the same time they're facing the uncertainty of starting a new job, moving to a new location, and dealing with post-college debts. "This is the end of an era," they say, and the nostalgia they're suffering includes fond memories of college partying.

"I CAN'T TALK TO MY *PARENTS* ABOUT SEX!"

Most of us find it easiest to avoid thinking or talking about either our parents' or our children's sex lives. Although students don't want to discuss sex with their parents, sex is one of the most important issues of their college years, and they *are* thinking and talking about it—a lot!

As easy as it is for your child to talk to friends about intimate experiences, it is exceedingly difficult for him or her to talk to you. Few parents know when their child has his or her first sexual experience, but the hope is that the first experience is a choice rather than "something that just happened."

When Cyl was home for spring break during her junior year, she mentioned to her mother, Joan, that she needed a formal dress. She had been dating her boyfriend for two months, and he had asked her to go to his fraternity's spring dance. The dance was off-campus, at a hotel ballroom downtown. "I don't want you to worry, Mom, but just so you know, everyone stays at the hotel after the dance. Honest, we're not doing anything wrong, but Gabe is twenty-one, so it's legal for him to drink. It's not like he'll get totally bombed, but we want to be safe, so we're going to get a room. Everyone's getting a room. It's not a big thing."

Although Joan's first instinct was to forbid her daughter ever to return to school, she took a deep breath and said, "Cyl, let's be realistic. You're planning to stay in a hotel room with a young man you like a lot. I think you need to acknowledge that you very well might have sex, or else you need to come up with a specific plan for *not* having sex—like getting a separate room for yourself. Please, don't put yourself in a situation where you end up sleeping together without actually thinking about it and planning for it. I just want you to make sure you talk about it so that you know what it means to each one of you, and you won't have any regrets later."

As Cyl stormed off, fuming that her mother didn't trust her, Joan worried that she had somehow just given her daughter permission to have sex with her boyfriend. A few hours later, however, Cyl came back and acknowledged that her mother was right. "I don't know if you want to hear this, but I think maybe I really do want to sleep with Gabe. He's the nicest guy I've ever met, and I like him so much. We haven't actually talked about it, but the truth is, I bought a package of condoms a couple of weeks ago, and I've had them with me just in case things went too far. You're right—I should talk to him about it, and if it's going to happen the night of the dance, I don't want either one of us to be drunk. I want it to be a good experience."

Cyl was fortunate that her mother was willing to confront the issue. For too many students, sex is unplanned or unwanted, or it's simply not thought through. And that can lead to regret, resentment, or unwillingness to take responsibility.

Students can find booklets and brochures at their college health service on just about any sex-related topic, but most students today prefer to begin their information search in private, on the Internet. As a result, many college health services now provide online Web sites with sex information, like Columbia University's Go Ask Alice (http://www.goaskalice.columbia.edu/).

WHEN GOOD TIMES GO BAD

Sometimes students don't have the opportunity to make their own choices. About 3 percent of college women experience an attempted or a completed sexual assault each year.[16] In the vast majority of cases, the assailant is a friend, classmate, boyfriend or ex-boyfriend, or acquaintance. Women believe they are safe, spending time with a friend, and they are unprepared when "things go too far." The majority of these assaults take place in the victim's own residence.

Because victims so often know their assailant, their reactions are complicated. They tend to blame themselves, thinking, "I must have made him think I wanted sex." They experience guilt, wondering if they could have done something to prevent the assault. They are confused about whether or not what happened was a rape, believing that since they let the person into the room, or they went somewhere willingly with the attacker, no one else would consider it an assault. Acquaintance rape, or date rape, is often minimized as "not a real rape." Victims decide not to report the assault, fearing either that their assailant will retaliate or that, by reporting the assault, they may ruin his reputation. They conclude that no one will believe them, thinking, "It's my word against his." If the student who was assaulted is gay, lesbian, bisexual, or transgender, there are additional concerns about being exposed, or "outed," if the assault is reported.

Students especially dread telling their parents about an acquaintance rape. They want their parents to believe they are responsible and safe. Acknowledging an assault may feel like revealing weakness or irresponsibility. They don't want their parents to be disappointed in them; if they think they could have or should have done things differently, they worry that their parents will have the same doubts. Students also know that their rape will affect their parents. They don't want to cause them shame or discomfort.

In many cases, by withholding the information about a sexual assault from you, your student is protecting herself or himself (because men, too, can be victims) from admitting what happened.

Jenna always had a very close relationship with her parents. "I never understood my friends who wouldn't tell their parents about the parties they went to or the boys they met. I told my parents everything!" But when she was sexually assaulted in her residence hall room early in her sophomore year, she did not tell her family.

It was Jenna's mother, Connie, who finally confronted the issue. "In retrospect, I should have known right away," Connie said later. "She came home one weekend unexpectedly, and she seemed so exhausted. She asked me to do her laundry and wash her sheets, and she went up to her room and slept. I thought maybe she was just tired—students always seem to work so hard, and they stay up late with their friends. But she slept almost the whole weekend, and when it was time to go back to school, she was so sad. She had always been anxious before to get back, but this time she seemed so unhappy—almost clingy towards me and her dad."

As the year progressed, Jenna seemed unsettled. She would call home and cry, fretting about noises outside her room or boys who made comments about her. She no longer talked about friends at school, and her grades were abysmal. At one point, Jenna mentioned to her mother that she didn't drink anymore because once, after she had been partying, she fell asleep and didn't wake up for sixteen hours. When she finally woke up, she couldn't remember anything.

Midway through the second semester, Connie happened to read a newspaper article about a college woman who had been given a date-rape drug. According to the story, some of the woman's sorority sisters noticed that she seemed disoriented and sleepy after only one drink. When she fell asleep and her friends could not wake her, they called an ambulance. The words on the page blurred as Connie began to recognize that her daughter had talked about some of the same symptoms the article described—confusion, exhaustion, memory lapse, and lingering depression. Had Jenna been drugged and raped?

Connie dug out the orientation materials from Jenna's college and found the school's rape crisis phone number. She talked to the director of the program, who advised her to encourage, but not force, her daughter to talk to a peer counselor. If Jenna wasn't yet ready to deal with the assault, she would not be able to discuss it. If she was ready, she may need only a gentle nudge.

Connie simply told Jenna, "I was looking through some information from your college, and there are peer counselors—students your age—who can talk about rape and sexual assault. It sounds like a good program. They have drop-in hours on Tuesday morning, so you could go in and talk to them. Would you do that?"

Jenna didn't argue or ask why her mother was giving her the information; she simply said she would go. And on Tuesday morning, she went.

Parents' reactions to their child's assault is intense. It feels like an assault on you. Jenna's father was incensed, and he was ready to pound on the young man's door and bodily remove him from the college. Jenna's mother, however, was more intent on taking care of her daughter. She encouraged Jenna to follow the advice of the rape counselor and file a petition through the registrar's office to have her grades for fall semester changed from letter grades to "pass." Connie urged Jenna to move to a different residence hall where she would no longer have to see where her assault occurred. The support of her family, including both the caretaking from her mother and the fierce loyalty of her father, gave Jenna the courage to work through the steps of the recovery process.

In Case of Rape: How a Parent Can Help

- First and foremost, believe your child when he or she tells you about a sexual assault. Talking about an assault is a critical step toward recovery, and it is very difficult for both the victim/survivor and the listener.
- Make sure that "first steps" are taken. Be certain that your child is no longer in danger. If the assault was recent, encourage your child to seek medical attention and support. Many colleges and universities have sexual assault support programs, and community sexual assault support services are also available.
- Avoid being overly protective or assuming a controlling role for your child. You cannot fix this; your child must do the work. You can, however, encourage your child to seek help, while recognizing that it may take time to muster the energy to move forward. The assault took away your child's sense of power, and it is critical for the victim/survivor to assume self-control again and to know that you support her decisions.
- Recognize your own feelings of anger and helplessness. You can find helpful information for yourself by checking your library for resources on sexual assault issues or by talking to someone at your local rape-counseling program. You can also contact the Rape, Abuse & Incest National Network (RAINN), 1-800-656-

HOPE, Extension 1, or check online at http://www.rainn.org.

- While you can offer to support your child as he or she presses charges or confronts the attacker, it is not your role to retaliate. Your child knows the situation best. In some cases, a victim may not be able or ready to confront the assailant; don't put your child in the situation where he or she is defending the attacker to you.

CYBERSTALKING

Harassment and stalking have long been problems on campus, but the wonders of technology have increased these problems by allowing new forms of harassment. Colleges require students to have e-mail accounts, and those accounts can be used for electronic stalking. What might seem like innocent, online flirting to the sender of a message may feel like intimidation to the recipient.

A freshman boy noticed an attractive girl one afternoon at a coffee shop and overheard her friend calling her Claudia. She left before he could gather the nerve to talk to her, but that evening, he checked the school's online directory for all the Claudias on campus. He decided she must be the Claudia who lived in West Hall, right across the street from the coffee shop. He sent an e-mail, asking if she had been at the coffee shop at 4 P.M. that afternoon, wearing jeans and an Old Navy sweatshirt and carrying a red backpack. If so, would she be there at the same time the next afternoon?

When she didn't show up the next day, he sent another message. "I'd like to meet you. I'll be in the lobby at West Hall tomorrow at 4."

To Claudia, the e-mails felt threatening. Someone she didn't know was describing her clothes and her movements. He had been able to find her e-mail address, and he knew where she lived. She contacted the campus police, who tracked his e-mail address and waited for him outside his classroom the next day. "You have crossed a line," they warned him. "We're not going to take action this time, because we don't think you understood exactly what you were doing. But in the future, don't use the campus directory or your computer account to meet up with people who don't know you."

Cyberstalking is not always an innocent misunderstanding. Electronic harassment is the newest weapon of spurned boyfriends or girlfriends. When a relationship is going well, students trustingly give their computer passwords to a new love. After the breakup, a savvy ex can intercept e-mails or change passwords. It's no longer rare for a student, after ending a relationship, to open up her e-mail account and find threatening notes or hundreds of spam messages. Women and men alike may find that their former friend has subscribed them to pornography listservs or posted their e-mail address on some unsavory Web site.

If you hear that your student is being harassed, encourage him or her to contact campus police. If the harassment or stalking is related to technology, the computer services office should also be notified. The first instinct might be to delete the message and hope nothing ever shows up again, but tell your student to save the message and forward it to a campus authority. Every college should have a policy addressing electronic harassment. Students can have their e-mail address or password changed, and the computer services staff will do their best to track messages back to the source.

DO THEY REALLY KNOW WHAT THEY'RE DOING?

College students, as a population, are bright, inquisitive adults, who have every resource available to make wise choices. Certainly, they arrive at college having heard the message that abstinence is the only sure method of birth control. In a variety of ways, college health services and residence hall programming offer information about abstinence, birth control, and sexually transmitted diseases and infections, in an ongoing effort to educate students about the risks of casual sex. How could any student possibly end up with a sexually transmitted infection or become pregnant?

All the sex education in the world, however, doesn't alter the fact that college-age men and women are sexual, sensual beings. They are biologically programmed to desire intimacy, and they are at a prime age for being sexual. Depending on the culture of the school or your child's group of friends, student attitudes toward sex may seem to you to be alarmingly impersonal or even cavalier.

Various surveys indicate that nearly half of all high school students have had sex and that 80 to 90 percent of college students say they have been sexually active.[17] While students seem to know the basic facts about sexually transmitted diseases and infections (STDs and STIs), many see the only significant danger as AIDS/HIV. As long as they're hooking up with good, clean college students like themselves, they think, they're going to be fine. Condoms will protect them from pregnancy and any weird diseases that might be lurking in this partner's distant past. They don't realize that condoms do not protect them from some of the most common STIs: human papillomavirus (genital warts), molluscum (virus-caused skin growths), and genital herpes (a recurrent skin condition in the genital area, caused by a virus). Some infections are caused by direct skin contact, oral sex, and mutual masturbation, not by body fluid contact.

Some parents would prefer that the message to college students be a one-word statement: Abstain. The mother of an incoming freshman criticized the orientation program at her daughter's college because a segment of the program included informational skits about sexuality, pregnancy, and sexually transmitted diseases. "If you tell these kids how easy it is to use birth control, you're really just telling them to have sex," she said. "Don't talk about these things, and they won't think sex is an option."

Many students do abstain, and they are increasingly finding support among friends for their choice. Nevertheless, whether or not universities (and parents) address intimacy issues, sex will be on the minds of students. The good news is, you still have some influence. Let your student know what your expectations are, and continue to encourage safe choices. And keep talking. Then, if the time comes when your child needs to tell you about a sex-related issue, talking will be easier for both of you.

Students struggle with telling their parents if they are planning to move in with an intimate partner; if they are taking a trip with someone; if there's a pregnancy, a sexually transmitted disease, or a dysfunction. They *will* let you know if they're planning to get married. They may tell you if they are gay, but for most gays, lesbians, bisexuals, and transgenders, telling family members is the hardest part of coming out.

ACKNOWLEDGING SEXUAL IDENTITY

It is not uncommon for gay students to recognize and accept their homosexuality during their college years. Any feelings of "difference" during high school might have been repressed and attributed to the challenges of fitting into a small community or to the growing pains of adolescence. At college, however, when students have a chance to examine their feelings in a new setting, they may come to realize that the feelings they have hidden or wondered about for years are part of their identity. They finally want clarity. To some extent, the realization feels as if a burden has been lifted. This is the answer to a long-perplexing question, but it brings a few new problems. How will friends and family react?

When Chris told his parents he was gay, his mother felt almost as much relief as he did. She had seen how unhappy and depressed he often felt, and she also saw that the cloud had lifted with his coming out. His father, on the other hand, was miserable. He went through every cliché—"You just haven't met the right girl." "It will pass." "Is this one of those college things? You'll change your mind when you get out in the real world." "Did *I* do something wrong? Was it your mother's and my divorce?" "Maybe I should have done more with you when you were growing up. I should have insisted you live with me, not your mother."

Nevertheless, he too saw that Chris was growing more confident and content with himself. Although he had trouble accepting that his son was gay, he could not imagine his life without Chris in it. "I'm not exactly happy about this," he told his former wife. "I can't help but hope that he'll change his mind, but I guess that's my problem, not his. Chris really *is* a great kid, and what I want most for him is to be happy. It does seem like a load is lifted from his shoulders these days."

Whether the subject is pregnancy, a sexually transmitted disease, or homosexuality, your child has probably rehearsed the conversation many times by the time you hear the words, "Mom, Dad, I need to tell you . . ." By revealing the hard truth to the people who love them, students are accepting their situation. Even if they have previously talked to a doctor, a counselor, or a friend, now that they are telling their parents, they are beginning to confront and adjust to the issues.

What your student tells you may conflict with everything you believe and everything you have hoped for for your child. You may not approve of your student's behaviors or the situation your child is in. You may be hearing something that forces you to revise how you have always looked at your child. Any objections you voice, however, will not change what your child is telling you. Any suggestions you make will not change the circumstances. These are the times when children need their parents more than ever to help them handle the situation, or at least to keep loving them.

Practice these steps in advance:

1. Listen.
2. Say "Thank you for telling me."
3. Ask how your child is feeling and if there's anything you can do to be helpful.
4. Say "I love you." Then be quiet again in case there's more listening you need to do.

QUICK TIPS FOR STUDENTS

Don't Be a Victim of Sexual Assault

- When you're preparing for a date, take care of yourself first. Have enough money to pay for your meal and transportation home, if necessary. Have a cellular phone or phone card in case you need to make a call.
- At parties or bars, keep a friend in sight. Watch out for each other, and check in from time to time to make sure you're both comfortable with how things are going.
- Trust your instincts. If you find yourself in a situation where something feels wrong, look for a way out of the situation— move closer to other people or seek out a safe way to get home.
- Don't ignore sudden feelings of mistrust just because you have known someone for a long time. You can't tell if a person has the potential to rape based on past behaviors.
- Never leave a drink unattended or accept a drink that you did

not see poured. Date rape drugs can leave you unable to protect yourself or unaware of what is happening to you.

- Take assertiveness training and self-defense courses. Passive and submissive behaviors can be dangerous. If you become frightened, do your best to be assertive. Speak loudly and firmly, or yell.
- If you are sexually assaulted, go to a clinic or emergency room immediately. You can decide later whether or not to press charges, but it is critical that you receive medical attention and caring support as soon as possible.

Don't Be a Rapist

- First, be respectful. Any time you are uncertain whether your partner is comfortable with your behavior, ask! You can simply say "Are you OK with this?" Assume that no means no. What's more, assume that "I'm not sure" means no.
- Recognize that your sexual needs do not give you the right to do whatever you want. Any sexual activity should be mutually desired. If the other person is not capable of making an informed decision, do not have sex!
- Know the definition of sexual assault. If you think a grope or "feeling someone up" is just innocent fun, you could be surprised. In some cases, you can be arrested for these actions.
- Drink responsibly. Nearly every sexual assault on college campuses follows drinking by one or both individuals. In addition, be aware of how alcohol affects you. If drinking makes you more aggressive, you could be in danger of sexually assaulting someone. Being drunk is not a defense for committing sexual assault.
- If your friend or roommate is sexually assaulting someone, do what you can to stop the assault. You can be charged with complicity if you know about an assault and fail to intervene.
- Be aware that committing rape has severe consequences. For

your victim, there can be years of emotional trauma, guilt, and fear. For you, sexual assault can lead to criminal charges, attorney expenses, and prison. For both of you, a sexual assault can result in disease, pregnancy, and social stigma. A few minutes of sex are not worth years of regret.

CHAPTER 7

Study Snacks and All-Nighters

Health and Wellness

A food services director polled students to find out which breakfast cereals they wanted in the campus dining centers. The top six choices: Cinnamon Toast Crunch, Lucky Charms, Golden Grahams, Frosted Flakes, Frosted Mini-Wheats, and Corn Pops.

Any college freshman can tell you about the daily food pyramid. Students know what they should eat, and they have heard more than enough about how a poor diet will affect their health. Nevertheless, it's a fact of college life: Sugar and caffeine form the foundation of the student food pyramid. Students also know the theoretical benefits of a good night's sleep and regular exercise, but sleep and workouts are the first casualties when a final exam is coming up, or a paper is due.

A steady diet of soda, candy, and chips provides quick energy, but not necessarily good nourishment or stamina for the long haul. Students might manage to stay up long into the night talking with friends or cramming for a quiz, but they make up for the late hours by dozing off during lectures or searching out a secluded library carrel for a nap between classes. With each passing week, they become more susceptible to whichever illnesses might be lurking around campus.

A HEALTHY START

As parents consider their child's college dining options, they are swayed by the most complete meal plan on the list. They want their child to eat three meals a day, and the full meal plan is the most economical choice. So why, parents ask, is there no meal plan that offers twenty-one meals per week?

Most colleges provide only two meals on Sundays—brunch and dinner—and increasingly, schools are eliminating the three-meal schedule on Saturdays. So parents select the nineteen-meals-per-week plan, and then two weeks after school begins, their child decides to cut back to the fourteen-meals-per-week option.

Very few college students can be classified as morning people. Typically, they prefer to sleep as long as possible before dashing off to class. Those with 8 A.M. classes don't have time for breakfast; those who sleep past nine o'clock have missed meal-plan breakfast. At best, breakfast becomes little more than a quick stop to grab a bagel and a banana. If you're hoping to ensure that your student has a decent start to the day, you might make a better investment by buying or renting a dorm-sized refrigerator and urging your child to shop regularly for milk, juice, and cereal.

While it makes sense to plan for two meals per day in the dining center, students often protest that they can't possibly eat there that often. "My lab class on Wednesday meets at noon, and the dining room is closed before I get back to the dorm." "It's absolutely *required* to have at least one burger a week at the campus diner." "I wouldn't force a dog to eat dorm food for every meal!"

College dietitians have made great strides in improving food service in recent years, and flexibility has become the watchword in meal plans. Students can select from a considerable range of choices at each meal. Salad bars are standard, and many cafeterias have sandwich, soup, or pasta bars as well. Vegetarians and vegans can find entrées that fit their dietary demands, or at least they should be able to build a meal around the hot vegetables, pasta, bread, and salad ingredients. Many cafeterias even make ethnic foods available on a daily basis.

Ethan's mother had dismissed his occasional grumbling about the food until one night, in the middle of the week, he showed up at home just as she was sitting down for dinner. "I borrowed my roommate's car so I could come home for some real food. I'm not going to eat another meal at the dorm!" he vowed. "It's disgusting. I swear, it's the same two choices every night. The vegetables are mushy, the meat is gray, and they even manage to mess up the orange juice. Most of the stuff has no taste at all, and if it *does* have a flavor, it's foul."

Food was one of the things Ethan's mother had been especially concerned about before her son started college. Ethan was one of those teenagers who ate steadily from the time he got home after school every afternoon until he finished his final bedtime snack. She had wanted to make sure he could have second servings and a range of options at each meal. She even made a phone call to the food service director during the summer, and she was impressed with his description of the dining center. Ethan's complaints didn't make sense, according to what she had heard.

Sometimes, when students complain to their parents about food, there are other, undisclosed issues. In Ethan's case, the real motive was that he wanted to move out of the residence hall. He had had an invitation from an upperclassman to sublet the second bedroom of an apartment near campus, but he knew his mother would object. She already had told him she wanted him to stay in the dorm another year. He also knew, though, that he could gain her sympathy by claiming the food was inedible.

Food gets the blame when students want to come home because of a boyfriend or girlfriend, when they want to join a fraternity or sorority, or when they're having roommate problems and simply don't want to stay where they are.

Using food as an excuse is a brilliant means of persuasion. What parent can ignore a fundamental requirement of life? A kid has to eat. If a student were to complain about a roommate, parents would suggest "Talk it over. Ask the hall director to help. Maybe it's partly your fault?" But few parents will tell their student to tough it out when they hear she is not eating. What's more, it's almost a form of flattery—your child likes your cooking, and nothing else can compare.

Admittedly, dishes prepared for a college dining hall will not taste like home cooking. Because of the range of food sensitivities and allergies among the college population, the recipes are generally not seasoned like home cooking. The student who is accustomed to having real butter slathered on fresh, al dente vegetables will surely find steam-table carrots and peas bland and unappetizing. At the end of most serving lines, though, a spice bar provides salt, pepper, herbs, Tabasco sauce, and other seasonings.

Complaints about the food provide students with a social bond. They can connect with each other through shared suffering, and caustic remarks about "mystery meat" or "spaghetti soup" provide easy conversation starters and sometimes lead to a spur-of-the-moment group trip for pizza or dessert.

There are cases, however, where the food sincerely is bad, and students' complaints are the first step toward improvement. An unskilled food service director may be revealed only if students speak out.

How do you determine if the problem is serious, or if it might be the first step in a request to move out of the dorm? Parents can ask their child what kinds of choices are provided: Are there salad and pasta bars? Is there at least one dish that's palatable at each meal? If a student takes an entrée and doesn't like it, can she go back for something else? If your student has dietary restrictions, has he talked to the dietitian about special meals?

Although in most cases, the food really is edible, anyone who has eaten in a college dining center understands that the prospect of pulling every meal, every day from a cafeteria line can be unappetizing. A trip through the serving line means making choices from dozens of options—which students demand—but the noise of hundreds of students talking, flatware chinking against plates, hamburgers sizzling, and the occasional breaking glass adds up to a constant din. Each meal becomes a sensory overload. Every now and then, a student needs the break of a solitary meal, eaten in front of the TV, or a quiet restaurant in off-peak hours with a good friend and lazy conversation. If you cannot add $10 or $15 to your student's budget for extra meals from time to time, encourage him to request the cafeteria's brown bag lunch occasionally, just to provide a break from the routine.

ALL WORK AND NO PLAY

Unfortunately, even students who eat three balanced meals a day can suffer physically. We've all heard of the "freshman 15," those extra pounds that students pile on by opting for spaghetti and bread sticks for every meal, rich lattes at the coffee shop between classes, and a bag of cheese curls before bed. It is a college ritual to go out for pizza on Sunday nights, and it's part of the daily routine to gather in the lounge for sodas several times a day. It may seem that walking to classes and carrying a twenty-pound backpack would substitute for a gym workout, but students can quickly get out of shape.

The habits of other students also have an influence; at some schools, fitness buffs are seen as "dumb jocks," and any time spent outside of the library or lab lowers a student's intellectual image. Even at a school like Ohio State University, where spectator sports are the center of the social system, less than half of the students find time to exercise regularly.[18]

As with most lifestyle issues, you cannot force your child to exercise, but you can point out opportunities, ask what sounds interesting, and encourage participation. The Ohio State study found that especially for women, family support served as an inspiration to go to the gym. Your own behavior is also influential. When you exercise regularly, your student sees that you value a healthy lifestyle and that you find ways to make it part of your regular schedule. You don't need to dwell on the importance of exercise, but you can talk about what you saw during your morning walk or mention that you stopped at the gym on the way home from work. You can also plan hikes and bicycle tours into your visits to campus or schedule a family ski trip during winter break.

WHEN THE FLU BUG BITES

It's a horrible feeling to have your child call home and say "Mom, I'm sick." Even if she only has a cold, and you know she'll be fine with a bit of rest, you will feel helpless and anxious.

Students share germs in all kinds of creative ways—curling up on the floor with a roommate's pillow, using the computer keyboard in the library, and picking the pepperoni off a friend's slice of pizza. One junior swears that she and all her friends contracted pinkeye by playing with her kitten. You can trust that every student will catch cold, come down with the flu, or at least have a headache at some point during the year.

You know your child, and you know if he tends to overdramatize when he's sick, or if he complains only when he is in serious pain. When you get a phone call asking for help, trust your instincts and rely on your longstanding routines, at least to the extent that long-distance communication allows it. A phone diagnosis doesn't permit you to confirm with a look or a touch just how sick your child is, and your student may not be able to relay satisfactory answers when you ask "Is your forehead hot? Are you flushed?"

When students call home to tell you they're sick, they are looking for the pampering they received as a child. They want to hear the advice they know you will provide: Go to bed, drink lots of juice, take a pain reliever, and heat up a bowl of chicken soup. They would like you to tell them how long it will be before they feel better. Just hearing the concern in your voice serves as a long-distance hug.

On the other hand, many students don't want to even acknowledge an illness. Students who are trying to establish independence believe that health problems might be proof that they can't take care of themselves after all. One young man suffered for weeks with an ingrown toenail, treating it with a topical ointment and hoping it would get better. He went to the health service only when his toe swelled so badly he couldn't stand to wear a shoe. A young woman with a rash on her buttocks was too embarrassed to tell anyone or make a clinic appointment. "It will just go away," she thought. After a month of itching, she had to acknowledge that it was much worse. She finally called her mother, only to receive the obvious advice, "Go to the doctor."

When a student is sick, the last thing she needs is the added stress of figuring out how to make a medical appointment and how to deal with health insurance. There are some things you can do *before* your child becomes sick or injured:

- Be sure that you and your student know what services are available on campus and when he or she should seek help off campus. Urgent care or weekend appointments, for example, might mean a visit to a local hospital.

- If your student is covered on your health insurance, he or she must know how to make a claim. Many family health insurance plans are tied to specific clinics or a provider area; coverage is different when the student is away from home. In some cases, co-payments are higher for care outside of the coverage area. Let your student know if he is required to call the insurance company before seeing a doctor.

- Give your child an insurance card with the coverage information and company phone numbers. If co-payments are required at the time of service, be sure your student has some emergency funds for only that purpose.

- Explain your family prescription coverage if you have it, and go over the information on how to obtain new prescriptions or refills.

- If your student uses eyeglasses or contact lenses, be sure he or she has a copy of the most recent eyewear prescription.

- Talk about dental coverage; for a student, a chipped tooth or broken filling is a devastating problem. If you have emergency dental care, be certain your child understands the coverage. Also, discuss whether your student would prefer to have regular checkups and cleanings with the hometown dental clinic during breaks, or if a campus-area dentist is preferable.

Health Kit

When your student is packing for college, provide a few of the first-aid basics, such as a box of tissues, a packet of bandages, and acetaminophen or ibuprofen. In addition, you can pack a health kit with instructions to open it only in case of illness. In the kit, pack more of the essentials—pain medication and tissues—along with some extra items.

Digital thermometer

Cough syrup

Throat lozenges

Favorite soup (in a format that is easily prepared in a residence hall)

Bubble bath

Tea bags

Jar of honey

Some of the comforts that worked when your child was small: kids' games, books, puzzles, comic books; coloring book and crayons; favorite videos (most college students like to revert to childhood activities from time to time)

A get-well card with a caring message, signed by family members

PREDICTING PROBLEMS

Cold and flu season hits campus about the time students are preparing for midterm exams. If shorter days and falling temperatures are not enough to dim the excitement of first-year students, upcoming tests are a reminder that college requires work. Students start pulling all-nighters and searching for the perfect formula to help them stay awake a few extra hours. In a show of camaraderie, upperclassmen pass along their recommendations to new students: You might be able to sleep through a psych lecture, but never doze off during chemistry lab. Mountain Dew has more caffeine than any other beverage in the study lounge soda machines. The purpose of study snacks is to keep you alert—try mixing equal parts of M&M's, raisins, and roasted whole coffee beans.

As immune systems are pushed to the limit, students start coming down with any passing illness. Then they postpone treatment until it's "convenient." Homework deadlines and tests are much higher priority than a cough or an ache. By the time they can work a call to the clinic into their schedule, they're miserable and hoping for an immediate appointment.

Freshmen are especially determined to tough out the misery, no matter how sick they may be. The first-year student who comes down with a case of mononucleosis midway through the first semester will not want to concede that she can't handle a full class load. She will struggle to attend all her classes, even if she falls asleep as soon as she sits down. After working so hard to get into college, waiting so long to arrive on campus, and dreaming so much of success, it is unfathomable that the need to sleep could squelch her plans.

Many of the peak periods for health issues are predictable. Students get sick just after they meet the deadline for a major project, and any class that includes public speaking will raise stress levels and lower endurance. Final exam week takes a lot out of students. Within a few weeks after a student moves into his first apartment, he might end up on the edge of malnourishment—the reality of meal preparation is harder than it seemed. And as the senior faces decisions about graduate school or job hunting, anxiety can lead to stress-induced health problems.

Parents feel torn between the desire to honor their child's desire for independence and the need to protect his health. In most cases, the role of parents during the college years is to support their students as they grow increasingly independent, not to make decisions for them. Unless the student is willing to grant permission, parents will not have access to health information about their child. Although colleges provide forms for release of financial and academic information to family members, they are more cautious about health records. A physician or a psychologist might encourage your son to tell you about a health condition, but she won't be calling you about the diagnosis and treatment options.

ILLNESSES TO WATCH FOR

As difficult as it is to entrust your child's well-being to health professionals you've never met, college health service staff are particularly skilled in diagnosing and treating those problems that are most likely to affect college-age students. Some mental and physical conditions are especially associated with young adults, and the nurses and doctors at the college clinic know what to look for. The short list includes mononucleosis, meningitis, eating disorders, and depression. The onset of asthma, diabetes, and schizophrenia can occur in this age group as well.

Mononucleosis

Every year, soon after classes begin, college health clinics expect to see a few cases of mono. Freshmen are especially vulnerable, and they are the most likely to minimize the early symptoms. Adjustment to college, change in diet, and lack of sleep all contribute to weakening the immune system and increasing stress levels. Students who ignore the early symptoms, believing "it's just a cold," end up exhausted and dehydrated, barely able to make it to the clinic for an appointment.

Meningitis

The first thing to remember about meningitis is that it is rare. Meningitis infects the membrane surrounding the brain and spinal cord, and it is usually caused by a viral or bacterial infection.[19] Viral meningitis is painful and often requires hospitalization, but it is much less likely than the bacterial variety to cause serious consequences. It is also not as easily spread from person to person. Bacterial meningitis is more contagious than the viral variety, and it can result in long-term health problems or even death.

Students who live in residence halls are statistically more likely than the general population to develop bacterial meningitis disease. Even compared with college students as a whole, those who live in dormitories are at greater risk.[20]

The conditions of residence hall living—close quarters, a population with stressed immune systems, and the tendency among students to overlook simple sanitation—happen to be the conditions that bacterial meningitis prefers. The bacteria spread when students share a soda or a kiss, or through contamination from coughs and sneezes. The early symptoms mimic flu or colds— headache, fever, sore throat, and nausea. One of the danger signs is a stiff neck and inability to bend the chin down to touch the upper chest. Because meningitis can progress rapidly, it requires a quick diagnosis.

The American College Health Association recommends that students consider being vaccinated against the disease. Not all health insurance policies cover the vaccine, but some colleges will provide vaccinations at no cost or reduced rates. Most parents, when they hear about the risk, urge their students to receive the vaccine.

Eating Disorders

Eating disorders are not confined to first-year students, but they may be exacerbated by the initial stress of leaving home. The complications of so many life changes at once can send students looking either for comfort or for something they can control. Either way, food takes over. When we think of eating disorders, we commonly think of anorexia and bulimia and their effects on women. College men are also affected by these conditions.

Anorexia and bulimia are insidious in that victims are so

deeply preoccupied by food, diet, and body image that there is no room in their thoughts to acknowledge the need for change. They have a goal in mind, and they are focused on all the minute details that will get them to the goal. Every day they count calories consumed, estimate calories burned, step on the scales to see if they're making progress, and endure immense guilt for any slipups.

Students who have experienced eating disorders during high school are especially at risk when they begin college, but anyone with an obsession about food may develop an eating disorder. In some cases, women in residence halls and sororities have taken bingeing and purging to the level of group activity. They might spend an evening gorging on snacks and then support one another as they justify the logic of getting rid of all those calories.

Eating disorders usually require some form of intervention and counseling assistance, but family and friends face a daunting task when they set out to help. These disorders are complex, and blame or criticism will only make things worse. Until victims want to change, they will find ways to continue their behavior. Unless your child is in imminent danger, the best you can do is point out what you are seeing, express your concern, and provide information on where to seek help.

For more information about eating disorders and the parent's role, check the following Web site: http://www.something-fishy.org.

Depression

Clinical depression is often first diagnosed in the late teens and early twenties, but to complicate matters, college students are living a lifestyle that contributes to depression. They are under constant stress, they don't eat healthy foods, they don't sleep regularly, and they don't exercise. They are judging themselves against their classmates, and they can always find someone smarter, more attractive, more outgoing, or thinner. Today's students have exceedingly high expectations for themselves, and few can meet their own lofty goals.

Depression *is* a concern among college students. You may need to worry if you see evidence that your child is pulling away from friends and family, using drugs or alcohol to excess, refusing to participate in favorite activities, or is feeling especially disappointed or dissatisfied with himself. If he has no energy to go to classes or leave his room, or if he is constantly exhausted, he needs to see a doctor for an evaluation.

Suicide is among the leading causes of death among college students.[21] Clinical depression, along with depression prompted by alcohol or drug use, a financial crisis, academic failure, the breakup of a relationship, trouble with the law, the death of a friend or family member, or issues about sexual orientation, can bring on suicidal thoughts. When students recognize that they are not meeting their own or their family's high standards, they can fall into an ever-deepening spiral of self-blame and shame.

Nevertheless, the occasional bad day is normal. As much as you hate for your child to be unhappy, students sometimes need to wallow in self-pity and misery for a few days or a week. Before you panic about your child's mood, look for evidence that he is making friends, attending classes on a regular basis, and participating in campus events. As long as your child is maintaining a normal schedule and can talk about activities, friends, and what's going on in classes, things are probably all right.

WHEN THE PROBLEMS ARE TOO SERIOUS TO IGNORE

It's difficult to decide when responsibility should revert to you. In most cases, the safest route is to present options and allow your child to make the final choices. If an injury or illness keeps a student out of the classroom for more than a week, he might want to consider dropping at least one class. We urge students to think about the kind of classes they are taking, and whether missed classes can easily be made up. Lecture classes and courses that rely primarily on reading and writing tend to be more flexible; students can work with an instructor to make up missed assignments. Language, math, or lab courses rely heavily on in-class learning. It's hard for a student to keep up with the material if several sessions are missed, and it is unfair to the other students in the class for the instructor to slow down the pace for one student.

Students worry that dropping a class means they will fall too far behind on the college schedule: "If I don't have 15 credits this semester, there's no way I can graduate in four years." "I can't drop physics—it's the first class in a two-year sequence, and I can only take it fall semester. I'll be a whole year behind."

Certainly, there are downsides to dropping a class, but overworking during a serious illness may result in poor performance in every class. Too many low grades can lead to academic probation; students who fail to fully understand the material in the first course of a sequence are likely to fail the next course. A dropped class might require a few months of summer school or even an extra year of college, but if it means success rather than failure, or health rather than lingering illness, the additional time is worth it.

In severe situations, parents do have the right to intervene. If your child is incapable of making decisions, or if you have good reason to believe that your student is suicidal, you will have to step in. Even some of the toughest advocates for student privacy will acknowledge that parents have the right to act if their child's life is in danger. If your child is talking about suicide, let her know that you are concerned, and encourage her to talk to a counselor or physician. If there is evidence that she has made a suicide attempt or is planning to harm herself, insist that she see a health professional. Take her yourself, or ask a college staff member to check on her if necessary.

MAKING A CLEAN BREAK—GOOD INTENTIONS CAN YIELD BAD RESULTS

If New Year's Day provides incentive to commit to new resolutions, the first day of college seems like an even greater opportunity for change. Every year, a new batch of freshmen promise themselves and their parents that they will become serious students, they will give up bad habits, and they will no longer fall into the slothful patterns of their youthful and ignorant past. Many students—with or without their doctor's advice—regard the start of college as a chance to try life without the medication, therapy, or support groups that have long been part of their normal routine. The young woman with a learning disability is tired of being labeled, so she refuses to register with the college disability office. The athlete who is sure that he now can concentrate on his studies neglects to have his prescription for Ritalin filled before he leaves for school. The student who thinks she has finally outgrown her adolescent depression stops taking her antidepressants.

When absolutely everything in a student's life is changing—where and how she lives, whom she lives with, even what she eats and how much she sleeps—this can be the worst possible time to give up the medications and support systems that have helped in the past.

In high school, Amy had signed up for a support group led by the school psychologist. Her parents' divorce had been hard on her. The sessions were often emotionally draining, but the group helped her find answers to many of her questions. As she prepared for college, though, she was well beyond the crisis, and she was relieved to think that she would no longer be going to group counseling every month. It felt like freedom—no more therapy!

A few weeks after Amy moved to campus, her mother became concerned about the tone of her daughter's phone calls. Amy sounded increasingly depressed and complained that she had no close friends. Her classes were hard, and she wasn't enjoying them at all. All she wanted was to come home.

Her mother urged Amy to talk to a counselor at the university, and after a few sessions, Amy began to see how leaving home for college had resurrected some of her anxieties related to the divorce. This time *she* was the one who had left home. She had never understood how her father could walk away from the family and start a new life; now she was doing the same thing. With a little help, Amy found ways to make a fresh start for herself and still keep room in her life for her mother.

It is understandable that students want a chance to give up those burdensome, long-term treatments or medications. Parents, meanwhile, are happy to see their child "move on with life." They want to believe that their son or daughter has overcome past problems, and college feels like the milestone that marks the cure. If the new challenges of college cause a recurrence of old illnesses or problems, though, parents are not there to notice the signs. Students may be the last to detect their own regression, and when they need help the most, they may be incapable of seeking it out.

College disability counselors sympathize with students who want to try getting along without extra support. They do not force students with minimal physical disabilities to live in handicapped accessible rooms, and they don't insist that students with learning disabilities must use special accommodations if they don't want to. If the student eventually finds that the extra assistance is needed, though, the disability office must have the paperwork and physician's reports documenting the disability. Similarly, the student who falls into depression but has allowed his medication to lapse will have to meet with a psychiatrist to obtain a new prescription. Students are wise to file the forms even if they don't think they will ever want the assistance.

The Boy Scouts motto, "Be prepared," is the best advice parents can give. Your child can be assertive about demanding a fresh start, but having all the appropriate health records on hand is a simple insurance policy. If the time comes that you get a sense your child needs the support systems or medications that have helped in the past, you can encourage him to visit the disability office or take the prescription along to a clinic appointment.

ROAD HAZARDS

Commuter students face few of the obvious health-related adjustments that residential living creates. They sleep in their own beds, eat home-cooked meals, and avoid the shared germs in dormitory rooms. When they're sick, they even have the caring attention of their family physician, as well as Mom and Dad. That does not mean, however, that commuters are risk free.

Research indicates that commuters are more prone to depression in college than residential students.[22] The commute itself contributes to the stress of school, especially in urban areas, and commuter students usually work more hours than residential students. Their schedules are segmented, and balancing work, home, and school can be exhausting. It's like living three separate lives, and commuters struggle to find enough time in the day to do justice to all the demands. What's more, the frustrations add up as they try to finish homework assignments between classes, only to find the books they need are at home. Or they plan to revise a paper over the lunch hour at work, but then remember their first draft is on their computer at home.

Even with parents on hand to oversee their health, commuter

students face considerable risks. Perhaps more than other students, they feel they don't have time to be sick. They push themselves beyond endurance and then find themselves multitasking in the car on the way to school—eating, drinking, and talking on a cell phone while hurrying to get to class on time.

Commuting students are convinced that no one recognizes all the stress and extra responsibility they face: "Everyone thinks my life is just like when I was in high school, but it's not! College is much harder, but because I'm living at home, no one notices the change."

Parents of commuters have a better chance than most to see when the demands are greatest and to find ways to ease the pressure. Ginny's mother offered to drive her daughter to campus during midterms and finals, giving her child a chance to study on the way to school and nap on the way home. When she picked her daughter up on the last day of finals, they went to dinner and a movie to celebrate. Neil's parents declared that Sundays meant absolutely no family obligations. He was relieved of all household chores at least one day a week, and his father made the commitment to wash and vacuum his car for him every weekend.

The greatest stress reliever for commuter students is for their parents to recognize that they are working hard and to step in from time to time and give them a break.

QUICK TIPS FOR STUDENTS

- "Prevention is the best medicine." You already know the basics: Eat some fruits and vegetables every day, drink plenty of juices and water, sleep at least seven hours a night, and exercise.
- Keep a cautious distance from friends and roommates when they are sick (but be kind—bring them soup from the dining

center and offer to pick up some juice and tissues from the convenience store). During cold and flu seasons, wash your hands more frequently.

- When you *do* start to feel sick, give yourself a break. Don't try to fight through the aches and pains. Take a nap; drink even *more* juices and water. Call the health clinic and ask for advice—should you make an appointment to see a doctor? Should you be taking any medication? Then follow their advice.
- Watch for signs of stress. If you notice that you frequently feel anxious or depressed, have trouble sleeping or can't seem to get enough sleep, lose your appetite or can't stop eating, or have persistent headaches or stomachaches, make an appointment to talk to a doctor.
- Colleges usually provide easy access to counselors and therapists. Use the resources!
- Alcohol, tobacco, and long weekends of partying take their toll on health. Look for less hazardous ways to have fun.

CHAPTER 8

Singing in Choir, Studying in Kenya

Learning Outside the Classroom

As high school juniors and seniors, most kids recognize that they can bolster their college applications by listing extracurricular activities. A balance of sports participation (the swim team) and intellectual achievements (the debate team or math club) indicates a well-rounded college prospect. Long-term participation in an activity shows commitment, so high school students may continue piano lessons long after they lose interest. Throughout the final year or two of high school, students rush from class to practice to a babysitting job, busy from breakfast until long after supper, with no break on the weekends.

By the time they arrive at college, then, some students are so burned out that they spend their entire first semester holed up in their dorm rooms, watching TV and listening to CDs. They tell themselves they can't get involved yet because they must concentrate on their studies. The truth is, they are relieved finally to have a moment to themselves.

Then one day, they emerge from their room, bored by too much free time and looking for something to do. The options now seem dizzying, and the selection process mystifying. "Student council was kind of fun in high school. How do I get into student government here?" "My philosophy professor said he advises the Chess Club. Maybe it would be smart to go to one of those meetings." "It's so amazing to watch the rowing team on the river in the morning. I'd like to do that!"

Experiences outside the classroom add value to what students are learning in their courses, helping textbook theory come alive. The sociology professor can lecture for weeks about group dynamics, but when students see firsthand how a few intensely competitive individuals can change the personality of the College Bowl team, group dynamics theory really starts to make sense.

SO MANY CHOICES, SO LITTLE TIME

Participation in clubs and organizations can help students clarify their career interests, providing the answers to lingering questions about an academic major. The student who discounted engineering as a career, believing it would mean a lifetime of working in solitude at a computer, finds that collaboration is a critical component in the engineering design process when he joins the school's solar vehicle team.

At the information fair during orientation, Bev tried to point her daughter toward the college newspaper's booth, but Lucy paused to look at the brochures promoting the Women's Center. "I don't think I want to work on the paper this year," Lucy told her mother. "It was fun in high school, but I heard it takes way more time in college. I'd rather try something different. Remember when I wrote that article last year on family violence, and I interviewed a girl whose family was staying at the crisis shelter? It says here that the Women's Center is looking for students who will train to be advocates for victims of violence. I think I'd like to look into this. I'm just going to ask a couple of questions, so maybe you want to go look at some of the other booths?"

Parents look through the lists of student organizations and see a number of groups that seem intriguing, some that raise red flags, and some that raise only questions. "Disc golf sounds like fun." "Why the sudden interest in NORML? Isn't that about reforming marijuana laws?" "How does a student choose from among the Aikido Club, the Karate Club, and Tae Kwan Do?" Parents can rarely predict which organization might make the most difference in their child's life—perhaps a group that addresses homosexuality, religion, or health and wellness topics.

The most successful and satisfied students invest time and commitment in their college. Generally, students join organizations because they have a particular interest, they want to meet like-minded students, or they are looking for personal or career development opportunities. In simple terms, they want to have fun. What they find in student activities are friends, recognition, fulfillment, and personal growth. The college becomes their home because they are making a commitment to some segment of the school through their involvement. They find their niche, their own small community within the larger campus.

All the benefits of campus involvement apply doubly to commuter students. Joining a club or organization helps commuters make and meet friends on campus; the newspaper office or the gym provides a place to hang out between classes. Membership in a group convinces the commuter that college isn't just a place to park the car and attend class; it's where he belongs.

Jillian's mother said that her daughter's entire outlook toward college changed when she joined the gospel group. "As a commuter, Jillian had trouble meeting people on campus until she made that connection. Rehearsals didn't start until 7 P.M., so she had to stay on campus after her last class. Within a couple of weeks, she was going out for dinner with some of the other singers before practice, and they have turned out to be some of her best friends. Music is not her major, she's actually a computer science major, but she says the gospel group is the best part of college."

The place to start getting involved on campus is wherever the student feels at least a little bit comfortable. Someone who enjoyed band or baseball in high school may not be headed toward a major in music or a pitching position on the college team, but he may still want to practice his saxophone or play ball. He can sign up for the pep band that performs for the women's soccer team or join an intramural sports club.

College activities offer a chance to try something a student might never previously have considered. A Midwesterner who enrolls at Stanford can sign up for the Surfing Association, and the Florida native at the University of Colorado can join the Ski Club. The sense of adventure and accomplishment that comes with learning a new skill or stepping into the unknown makes participation all the more fun.

Students can also find opportunities that don't require a long-term commitment, or in some cases, not even much personal effort. They shouldn't feel that every activity must have a life-altering outcome. A one-session campus workshop might offer lessons in papermaking or pot-throwing, but it may never lead to a decision to join the Art Club. The Film Society offers weekly entertainment for the entire campus, although only half a dozen students might be involved in the selection and programming.

Often, a student's personal skills and talents provide an unexpected opening into involvement opportunities. Experience in Web design might be exactly what the Law Club is looking for in its efforts to update its online image. Artistic ability may be the inroad to the Political Science Club, which needs "Get Out the Vote" posters for the coming election.

Ideally, the first year of college is a chance to sample the opportunities and begin to make choices. Students should try different groups with the idea that they are under no obligation to commit long-term. The second year is a time to sort through the previous year's experiences and determine which groups hold the most appeal. As interests and abilities change, students may find a new group that turns out to be the best fit yet. As sophomores and juniors, they might begin serving in leadership positions or at least doing more of the active work of the group— helping schedule games and select equipment for a sports club or recruiting new members and organizing readings for the Literature Club. As upperclassmen, students can shape improvements for the future of the organization and encourage emerging leaders. At any point in their academic career, though, students should have some idea of what skills they are learning or what they are gaining by being involved with a group.

"YOU'RE INVITED . . ." IS IT AN HONOR OR A SCAM?

Soon after grades were posted from fall semester, Shannon received a letter saying she had been selected to join an honorary society. "You're one of the best! Because your grade point average puts you in the top 10 percent of your class, you qualify for this great honor," the letter explained. Membership costs were "only $60 a year," and Shannon would be eligible for "lifetime benefits," which seemed mostly to be the right to list the organization on her résumé. "You will stand above the crowd when you apply for scholarships, graduate school, and jobs."

Students are flattered by invitations from honorary societies and selective organizations, but the question is whether such memberships make a difference to employers or graduate schools. If the group is affiliated with the student's college major, it probably is a commendable recognition to be invited to join. If it is a national organization, the value of the group depends primarily on the strength of the local chapter. If the local chapter is not active, the "honor society" could simply turn out to be good business for a few enterprising students who collect a portion of the membership fees from anyone they can enlist.

When it comes to scholarships, jobs, or graduate school, listing the name of an honorary society may not make a difference. It will help if the group has a historically prestigious reputation, such as Phi Beta Kappa, and it will certainly be useful if the student can elaborate on his or her contribution as a member. When students can talk about their role in planning or organizing events, serving in a leadership position, or participating in some other active way, the value of their participation becomes clear.

Before joining any group, and especially before joining a local chapter of a national organization, students should do some searching to find out about meetings and activities. The student can call a local contact person to ask about campus activities and plans for the upcoming year. If no meetings or activities are scheduled, the student is unlikely to gain much benefit by joining. Some honorary societies provide community service opportunities, schedule workshops and mentorships, and sponsor national conferences on leadership or career development. A national organization should have a Web site with information about its overall mission and goals. Decisions should be based on how the group fits with the student's interests, not on the name of the organization and flattery.

SEE THE WORLD . . . BUT LEAVE MY FRIENDS?

At the annual student activities fair, a crowd of eager questioners surrounds the table hosted by the International Studies office. A glance at the crowd's appearance, however, reveals more Hush Puppies than ankle tattoos, more worry lines than nose rings.

It's not that international study attracts only conservatives—the group is made up almost entirely of parents.

Ironically, parents and university staff tend to be more enthusiastic about international study than students are. Every parent has an idea of what study abroad will offer his or her student, and that image usually includes the art museums of Paris, the theaters of London, and the archaeological fields of Italy and Greece. Faculty and staff see international experiences as the ideal illustration of all they are trying to encourage: independence, accomplishment, and problem solving.

For many students, the idea of international study only conjures up images of a semester away from friends, an interruption to a budding romance, and the hassles of subletting an apartment in the middle of the year. Those students who decide to take the risk, however, almost always come home with visions of going abroad again, "It was the best thing I've ever done," they rave. "It changed my life."

Short-term study-abroad programs allow wary students to sample international opportunities without making a semester-long commitment. In many cases, the short-term programs whet a student's appetite for more. A three-week program, guided by a faculty member from the student's major, often is the prelude to a semester overseas a year later.

Both short- and long-term programs are available that support specific academic majors, allowing students to earn architecture credits through a program in Italy or business credits at a university in Australia. Other programs will offer general education courses in art history, political science, and literature through an exchange program in London. Students need to work with their academic and study-abroad advisers as they think through the academic requirements they can earn that will fulfill graduation requirements.

A first step in thinking about an international study program is asking the following questions:

- What part of the world do you want to visit?
- Do you have the language skills, financial means, or personal skills to be comfortable and successful while you're there?
- How long do you want to stay?
- What classes will you be taking? How many credits will apply toward graduation? How will this contribute to your education?
- How will the program advance your career goals? Personal goals?
- How will the cost of study abroad compare with staying on campus?
- Where will you live while you're there? On a campus, in a family home, in an apartment?
- Who will help you if something goes wrong?
- How will you communicate with your family and friends while you're gone?

The cost for a semester's study abroad can range from a little less than what it costs for a semester at the home college to double that amount. Although you don't want to go deeply into debt for your child's study-abroad experience, students should not try to make do on a completely bare-bones budget. The student who lives in London for three months and cannot afford an occasional half-price theater ticket or train fare for a day in Brighton will be frustrated by missing some of the obvious benefits of the trip. One of the common problems for students, though, is piling up credit card charges while they are abroad. They learn that their college in Paris is just a few hours from London and Brussels, or it's just a day trip to the south of France. Every weekend they're on a train for a new destination, and since "this is the chance of a lifetime," they buy a ring in Amsterdam or a watch in Germany.

Clear communication about finances is critical before your student leaves home, and parents should be alert to evidence of overspending. You can't blame your child for wanting to buy holiday gifts or a memorable souvenir overseas, but the debts that mount up while he's gone can take years to pay back.

Study abroad has particular benefits for commuter students. Beth lived at home during her freshman and sophomore years, but the first semester of her junior year, she signed up for a program in Spain. Besides giving her a chance to work on her Spanish credits, this was the first time she had lived with students her own age. "It was hard at first to figure out how to manage my time," she said, "but it was so much fun to live with friends who would ask me to go out with them, or we would just sit around and talk for hours on end. We argued sometimes, but we got over it. We had to—we shared a bathroom and kitchen, so we couldn't exactly avoid each other. The whole experience of studying abroad was great, but living with other students was, for me, the most important part of the program."

THE LONG-DISTANCE GOOD-BYE

Even those parents who have sent their child to a college or university halfway across the country will find it hard to put their student on a plane to go overseas for four months. All her belongings must be reduced to what she can carry. You didn't get a chance to scope out the campus this time; you have no idea what kind of living conditions she will face. What if something goes wrong? What if she needs you?

When Risa's mother first heard about her daughter's international study plans, she could only hope that Risa would remain in her room the whole time she was gone. Her mother always imagined her daughter would go to Mexico or Spain, where she could use her Spanish skills. Instead, she signed up for a program in Ghana, in northwestern Africa.

"Why Ghana?" her mother asked. "What do you know about Ghana? Is it safe? I don't even know what language they speak there."

"This program is perfect for me. After I finish my undergraduate degree, I want to apply for graduate school in public health," Risa explained. "In Ghana, I can do an internship with a community health program and get some really good experience. My classroom credits will count for my undergraduate degree, and the internship will help me get into the grad program I'm looking at."

An Internet search provided Risa's mother with reassurance that the University of Ghana was an accredited school with an excellent reputation. Her daughter would be studying with other Americans, and her classes would be taught in English. She would have advice and assistance from study-abroad staff in case of any problems. What's more, this program would cost about the same as a semester at Risa's own college.

International acts of terrorism in recent years have made parents cautious about study abroad. "I'm not putting my son on a plane to fly across the ocean," one mother told me a month after the World Trade Center attack. "How do I cancel him out of the program?"

Colleges and universities promote international study as one of the most important ways to increase global harmony. American students who spend time in other countries come home with a better grasp of the connections between cultures and economies around the globe. But is it safe?

Advisers of reputable programs do not recommend study abroad in any area they deem dangerous, and they will provide thorough background information on the culture and political climate of the land students will be visiting. Staff members will be on site to explain local and international issues and to provide assistance in case of an emergency. They will instruct students on how to maintain a respectful demeanor, keep a low profile, and take reasonable safety precautions wherever they study.

Parents can worry themselves sick over all the possible (but unlikely) problems, but a bit of careful planning will take care of most troubles.

- Make sure to confirm current travel safety information at http://www.travel.state.gov and health information at Centers for Disease Control and Prevention, http://www.cdc.gov.
- Be sure your student is aware of the medical requirements advised by his study abroad program. Program advisers should be working with students on immunizations and other preparations appropriate for the destination.
- Be certain that your student will have health insurance coverage overseas. Some insurance policies will not cover international medical care or emergency transportation back to the United States. If the study-abroad office provides an insurance policy, compare it with your own to make sure your student has adequate coverage. Ideally, your student will have a policy that covers family emergency transportation (to allow a family member to travel to the destination in case of serious illness or accident) and emergency medical evacuation (to bring the student home if necessary).
- Have your student assign power of attorney to you or another responsible adult for the time he or she is overseas. It's hard for students to give up their newfound status as adults, even temporarily, but power of attorney allows you to take care of those transactions your student may not be able to handle from afar—financial aid, banking, insurance, and income tax filing.
- Be sure your own passport is valid and up-to-date. In case of

an emergency, you will not have time to renew or apply for a passport.

- Make arrangements for discount rates on international telephone calls. A minor problem for your student, such as lost luggage, can result in lengthy phone calls and astronomical phone bills. Some long-distance phone services provide inexpensive rates for collect international calls. Be sure that you and your student understand the calling procedures and limitations in advance. Many discount programs will cover your child's calls to your home phone number but not to your work phone or other numbers.

If serious problems arise during a study-abroad experience, they are most often the result of a student's poor choices. A nineteen-year-old can drink alcohol in Europe, and the freedom of finally being able to drink legally leads to excess. Europeans, however, have little tolerance for Americans who are drunk. Students can find themselves in trouble with their hosts or confronted by police for alcohol abuse.

Students who are arrested for drug use while abroad can end up in jail. Before they go, students will hear from their study-abroad advisers about the laws in the country where they will be, but students don't always heed the warnings.

Academic failure is also a factor. Students believe that their work will be judged less critically when they are studying abroad. "The professors know we're not going to study," they think. "They'll take into consideration the fact that we're here for the total experience." European universities have somewhat different teaching styles, however, and a student may find his courses more difficult than at home. The temptation to skip classes is strong. "When will I ever have the chance again to go to Oktoberfest in Munich?" the student thinks as she cuts classes to travel. A week later, walking past a travel agency, she sees a sign that announces "Bargain Rates to Malta!" and plans another trip. Classes become low priority among all the tempting alternatives.

DEALING WITH THE UPS AND DOWNS

After Naomi received her acceptance letter for a summer study-abroad program to Turkey, she called home to tell her parents the exciting news. "This is going to be so great! I can't wait. I wish I could leave tomorrow!"

A week later, she was on the verge of canceling out of the program. "I can't go to Turkey! It's about 110 degrees there in the summer. I don't much like Turkish food, and I'm not sure they treat American women very well. What was I thinking?"

Studying abroad can be exhausting. By the time your daughter figures out the phone system or finds an Internet café where she can finally send you a message, she is likely to be tired, homesick, and depressed. Just as you did during those first phone calls home during the freshman year, you will hear about all the horrible experiences she is suffering. You will want to rush to her side or wire funds for a return ticket right away.

Keep in mind, though, that your child has already made some significant strides. She did, after all, search out a phone or computer, and she figured out how to use it. That probably meant that she first had to find a shop that sells phone cards and use foreign currency to buy one or figure out how to pay for computer access. The small accomplishments that meant little or nothing back in the United States feel like major achievements in a new land.

When they are in a new setting, students establish routines quickly to help them feel more comfortable and in control of their environment. They are compulsive about checking for their keys before they leave the house in the morning. A daily trip to the greengrocer to choose fresh vegetables becomes a ritual. They will make special efforts to board the same bus each day in order to see a familiar face in the driver's seat.

As life falls into a pattern, they begin to feel more competent and secure. They find that they are adjusting, and with every new success, they continue to gain confidence. They learn that local residents can understand them, even if their grammar and diction are not perfect. Instead of the embarrassment they suffered when they first tried to order a cup of coffee, they can now laugh at themselves when they realize they just asked to buy a newsstand, not a newspaper. They dare to make mistakes, and they find ways to correct their errors. Few educational opportunities provide such enlightening and gratifying experiences as study abroad.

When students return from study abroad, they are likely to face culture shock as they readjust to life at home. They have new thoughts on what is truly important. They may resent Old Navy stores, where they once bought all their clothes; now they cling to the shawls or skullcaps they picked up on market day in the village. They scorn the evening TV newscaster, challenging his comments about world affairs. They talk for hours on end about the people they met and the places they visited—or they sit sullenly in front of the computer, writing poetry or journaling about their time abroad.

Students are changed by international travel, and they typically believe that friends and family cannot possibly understand what they have gone through. They are more critical, more serious, and more reclusive for a time. Negative comments about home and American culture are common when students first return, but they will subside with time.

You can help make readjustment less difficult by looking at the photos with your student and encouraging him to talk about his experiences. Ask about those routines he established—what foods did he like? Who were the people he saw daily? Where did he go to study? As you listen, you will see how your child has changed and grown.

STUDY ABROAD—AN EDUCATION FOR THE FAMILY

Your interest in your child's destination can make the journey more exciting and more educational for your student. As Mother's Day, Father's Day, or your birthday approaches, suggest that the gifts you most want are a map and a tour guide of the area where your child will be. You can use the map and guide to learn about the area before she leaves, and while she is abroad, you can see where she is living and traveling.

When students are overseas, especially in a country that is very different from home, it can be almost impossible for them to figure out how to talk about their experiences. When students call home, parents can help by asking questions that put information into a familiar context. "I went to the farmers market in town this morning, and I was curious—are there outdoor markets where you are? Where do you buy vegetables?" "I'm sure there are no Baptist churches where you are—have you learned anything about how people worship?"

The more you know about your child's destination, the more you will want to explore it for yourself. Seeing your student function in a different culture can be one of the most gratifying experiences of parenting a young adult. Knowing that your son has mastered the train system of Russia or your daughter can read a ferry schedule in Greek is heartwarming proof of your child's intelligence, maturity, and independence. When you share some of your child's experience, it becomes more real and comprehensible to you—something you and your student can talk about and relate to in the months and years to come.

If you decide to visit your student during her international experience, however, assure her that you will not interrupt her academic schedule. Most study-abroad programs require students to be in class or working on projects a large part of the time. If she has tea with you after class, she may need to spend the evening doing homework. And students need time with their classmates—as study-abroad participants, they are all working through the same issues, and the support they offer each other is invaluable.

Still, a well-timed visit from parents is welcome, especially when students are aching for the sound of a familiar accent or wishing they didn't have to miss the holidays at home. By following a few guidelines, you can make a family visit rewarding for you and your child:

- Do not visit during the first few weeks of the program. Students need time to adjust and adapt to their new surroundings. Also, avoid visiting during the last days of the program. Exams, packing, and spending time with friends will fill their days as the program draws to a close.
- If you can schedule your arrival for a weekend, your child won't immediately have to choose between you and classes. Be prepared for role reversal while your child takes the lead, showing you where things are and how things work.
- Keep in mind that you may be on vacation, but your student is not. Do some exploring on your own.
- If you plan to tour with your child as a follow-up to her international study, let her finish the program before you arrive. And be prepared for some letdown after she has said good-bye to her classmates or hosts.

Domestic Alternatives

For the student who is not comfortable with the concept of international study, many of the same benefits are available without crossing an ocean or even using a passport. National college exchange programs let students spend a semester or a year at another college within the United States or in Canada. The University of Oklahoma student who always wondered about New England can spend a year at the University of Maine and get the best of both schools. Students can learn about different cultures by doing an internship on a reservation in New Mexico or a work project in Harlem; they can study French in Quebec or Spanish in El Paso.

Students can also explore the unknown in their own backyard. A student attending a school in a large city can tutor recent immigrants who are learning English; a whole new culture is just a bus ride away.

LEARNING BY DOING: COMMUNITY SERVICE

Your son mentions that he is earning credit in his nutrition class by packing box lunches for an AIDS organization, and you can't help but wonder: Whatever happened to lectures and exams? Your daughter calls home to say she's raising funds for the homeless by living for a week in a refrigerator carton. She's probably thinking this will be a great time with good friends for a noble cause. You're probably worrying about her safety, her studies, and her sanity.

More and more, colleges and universities are incorporating service learning and community projects into the curriculum. A pre-law class might include helping Somalis study for a citizenship test. An accounting course might involve setting up a budget for a nonprofit community organization. A women's studies class might ask students to interview women in local politics.

A good service learning project will not only provide opportunities for students to examine real-life situations, it also will include discussion and reflection on what students are observing. As a student's idealism faces off against some of life's reality, an instructor or adviser should be talking to him about his impressions and emotions related to the project. Frequently, students are asked to write a journal of their activities and reactions, and those impressions are shared with the instructor and classmates. The responses from other students can be particularly reassuring and supportive as individuals recognize that their reactions are not so unusual.

If your student tells you he will be doing a service learning project, there are some points that he should be able to discuss:

- How do students get to the site? How will they get home?
- Is there supervision at the site? What kind of support and guidance do students have from a faculty member or adviser? If there are problems or questions, whom will students talk to?
- What are the goals of the project? What is the student role in the project?
- What is the outcome (a report, a journal, a proposal for change)?

For more information on service learning, check out http://www.servicelearning.org.

QUICK TIPS FOR STUDENTS

- As they told you at orientation, join something! Try one safe bet—something you liked in high school. If you enjoy sports, check out what's available at the campus gym; if you were in the orchestra, find out if there's an ensemble group you can join. Also try one completely new activity. Can't find what you want? Ask your academic counselor for a suggestion, or ask your hall adviser if there's something you can volunteer to do in the dorm.

- If the group you join isn't as interesting as you thought, quit. If someone tries to pressure you to stay, make your decision based on what's right for *you*.

- Don't overcommit. It is important to be involved, but it's easy to get sucked into too many activities. Classes come first; then save time for studying and for being with friends. Clubs and sports should be fun; they should not add to the stress in your life.

- Service learning projects give you a chance to use the information you're learning in class, and they help you become comfortable in the community. There are great benefits to getting off campus and meeting the people who live nearby.

- Think about studying abroad. Most students discover it's the best thing they've ever done. Yes, it's hard to leave your friends, and there's the problem of leaving your dorm room or apartment for a semester. But you won't be the first person to study abroad, and someone on campus can give you some ideas for dealing with the details. Before you sign up for a program, get lots of advice, talk to your study-abroad office, and check in with your academic counselor to make sure you stay on track to graduate.

CHAPTER 9

"You Pierced *What?*"

When Social Choices Clash with Family Values

I n early November, Sharon drove to campus to bring her daughter home for a weekend visit. When Carla came to the residence hall lobby to meet her, Sharon had to look twice to recognize her, and she worked hard not to show her dismay. She had not seen Carla in two months, and she had had no warning that her daughter had dyed her hair ink black. Worse, it was now chopped short on just one side, revealing a row of silver hoops lining her right ear. Carla was wearing a long black skirt that looked as though it had seen years of wear, although it had never been part of Carla's high school wardrobe. The cute, brightly colored parka Sharon had bought before Carla went to school had been replaced by a shapeless floor-length wool coat, and Sharon could track her daughter's footsteps by the clopping of her heavy, thick-soled boots as she dashed down the hall to say good-bye to friends.

The ride home wasn't at all what Sharon had been looking forward to. She had imagined a long, pleasant conversation about Carla's classes and dorm life, but as soon as they got in the car, Carla asked if her mother minded if she took a nap. "I had two tests and a paper due today, so I didn't get much sleep the past couple of nights." Then she slumped down in the seat and closed her eyes.

When they arrived at home, Sharon fixed a quick dinner. As she offered Carla a taste of the pasta sauce, she spotted a round gold stud piercing her daughter's tongue, and she flinched with disgust. All her questions came out in one loud burst of angry disapproval. "What have you done to yourself? Have you punctured every part of your body? These clothes—where did they come from? And that hair! Don't you have any respect for yourself?"

Although Carla's new look was a huge surprise to her mother, it didn't seem particularly dramatic to Carla. When they both had calmed down enough to talk, Carla reminded her mother that she began college with two piercings in each ear and that Sharon had signed the permission forms for those when Carla was in high school. Adding four more to one ear didn't seem like a big issue.

During weekend trips to campus-area thrift shops with some friends, Carla had gradually built up a new collection of clothes. "And they hardly cost anything at all. You can get some real bargains at thrift shops, you know." The hair was a Halloween-weekend makeover, and she decided she liked it enough to keep it for a while. She admitted that the tongue piercing might be significant, but compared to the people she lived with, it wasn't all that unusual. On her floor in the residence hall, Carla said, there were at least six kids with nose rings. "Everyone has a pierced navel," she said, adding that a couple of students had pierced lips.

"Now, pierced lips," Carla said. "*That's* weird."

ADJUSTING WHEN YOUR CHILD COMES HOME

Parents are shocked by how quickly students change once they get to college. For many students, the first semester of college is as much about experimentation as it is about education. In high school, students may have avoided anyone who seemed strange. Now, living alongside dozens of new people, they find the differences engaging. They decide that the star athlete who, a year ago, would have seemed so arrogant is actually a lot of fun, and the eccentric who once might have seemed so unapproachable has a wonderful, wry sense of humor.

In some ways, it's like middle school all over again—a chance to try on different personas to see what fits. A student can adjust his image entirely from one day to the next, dressing in artsy black for a poetry reading on Tuesday evenings, wearing a business suit for an internship in town on weekday mornings, and painting his face in school colors for the game on Saturday afternoon. And in each transformation, he can still be himself and still be surrounded by supportive friends.

Major family issues crop up during the first visit home after a student goes to college, over winter break when the student is home for more than just a long weekend, and during the summer following the freshman year. Both you and your student will have your own expectations of how the weekend or the vacation visit will go, and your ideas will conflict. You might have made plans to stop at a nice restaurant for dinner to break up the ride home, but when you get to the dorm, you see that your son and his roommates are just finishing off the last of a three-foot submarine sandwich. You have invited Grandma for dinner, but your daughter has made arrangements to go out with a friend from high school: "I absolutely *have* to talk to Angie. We haven't seen each other in months. I promised I'd call her the minute I got into the house."

You have been looking forward to having your child home again, but after a few days, you find yourself incredibly annoyed at her behavior. "She hasn't picked up a single dish, she doesn't have time to help with anything around the house, and she's completely self-absorbed. She acts like God's gift to the family. How did I raise such a spoiled princess?"

Meanwhile, your student is baffled by her emotions at being back home. The family is not like what she remembered. Things feel different because things *are* different. She notices that you seem to be closer to her younger sister than you used to be, and her brother is talking about neighbors she's never even heard of. Or you moved the big TV into your bedroom and the little TV into the kitchen, so if she wants to watch a program, she has to sit at the breakfast counter.

She refuses to revert to the teen rules of reporting where she's going and when she'll be home. You want her to fit back into the family; you don't have any intention of treating your child like a guest in her own house. She, however, wants you to convey that her visit home is special. "You *said* you missed me. I thought you'd be glad to have me back! I didn't know you just wanted somebody around to do the dishes for you," she says. And you, meanwhile, don't understand why the only thing she seems to appreciate about being home is the bathroom.

ADJUSTING WHEN YOUR CHILD LIVES AT HOME

If your student lives at home and commutes, the evolution is no less troubling—it may be even *more* difficult because the whole family will be living with the adjustments on a daily basis.

Like Carla, Janet's son took to buying clothes at thrift shops during his first few months at college. Instead of his former standard outfit of jeans and a sweater, he was now wearing dark turtleneck shirts and black pants. One weekend, he hauled several boxes of his old clothes down to the basement.

"I don't have room for these clothes," he said. "I'm moving my bookshelves into the closet. I found a couch at a yard sale, and I'm putting it in my room. I need a place to study."

It wasn't just the clothes and the redecorating that bothered Janet. Her son had been a fairly traditional high school student—

participating in the track and cross-country teams, involved for two years with the debate club, taking a minor role in each of the class plays. Now it seemed as if he had no interest in sports, and all he talked about were music and movies. When she heard him on the phone with his friends, the conversations were all about musicians and film directors. He also began coming and going at odd hours.

One night she wasn't sure whether he had even come home. When he showed up for dinner the following evening, Janet confronted him. "You can't stay out until all hours like this! This is still my house, and as long as you live here, you have to follow a few rules."

"Mom, I'm an adult," he said. "Most kids my age don't see their parents from one holiday to the next. You can trust me. I don't want to have to keep you posted all the time."

It's not living away from home that changes college students. All their lives, children gradually move away from their parents. College coincides with the time in a child's life when he is taking bigger and bolder steps on his own. A child's separation from his family is a necessary step in the growing-up process.

While it's true that you have the right to establish the rules in your own home, you also need to recognize your child's increasing maturity and all the obligations in his life. A student's social commitments are interwoven with work and school. Study groups, going out with friends, and dating are all part of the package.

When your student is at home, you want to rely on him for a few basic family responsibilities. A family dinner on Sunday seems to you like a tradition, not an imposition. From your student's standpoint, it feels like one more obligation in an already overplanned schedule. Nevertheless, while you must sometimes accept the demands on your student's schedule, you can also request some family participation and basic respect.

Avoiding the Mishaps of the Student Visit

- If you will be picking up your student from school, clarify what time you will arrive and what time you expect to start home.
- Talk to your student about how much he expects to bring home. You might be thinking it's just a brief visit, so he should be able to fit everything into a duffel bag. He might have saved up a month's worth of laundry, and he may be planning to bring home his computer, stereo system, and all his CDs.
- Allow some time for helping your child pack the car, as well as some extra time for students to say their good-byes.
- Since the days leading up to school vacations are usually hectic, don't be surprised if your child sleeps all the way home. Once she gets home, she might sleep more than seems normal. There are valid reasons why students spend long hours in bed: they are exhausted by dorm life and exams; it feels comfortingly safe to be back in their own bed, in the security of their home and family; and retreating to bed is a way to gradually work back into the rhythms and pace of being home.
- Talk in advance about family obligations and how you will handle use of the car, curfews, and information sharing. Explain the reasoning behind your rules. Many parents find it's easier to say when they expect their car home rather than when they expect their child home.
- Discuss your expectations regarding doing your child's laundry, what daily household chores you want help with, and any family obligations or holiday plans. If you ask what plans your student is making, explain that you want to know so that you don't make arrangements that will conflict with his schedule.
- Recognize that some of his disagreeable behaviors are not a rejection of you and your values, but they serve as a way for him to communicate his independence.

CULTURE CLASH

Education is not only about gathering facts and theories. It's also about integrating lessons into life. Students are opening their eyes and their minds to the ideas and lifestyles of the friends they're meeting, the professors they're hearing, and the authors they're reading. Inevitably, they will begin to see their own experiences and their family's values in new ways.

The beliefs and practices that they have always taken for granted are challenged during the college years. Whether the doubts students express are about the religion they were brought up in, the family's politics, or their parents' economic status, parents can hardly help but feel threatened. It is painful to have your child question or challenge your beliefs, and it is frustrating to see her take on behaviors you had not expected.

Scott Slattery, a counselor and psychologist at the University of Minnesota, suggests that parents treat their suddenly unfamiliar student as they would a foreign exchange student.

"If you had a student visiting from Eastern Europe or Northern Africa, and he wore strange clothes, had a nose ring, or an unusual hairstyle, you probably wouldn't be offended," Scott says. "You might think it was all quite interesting. You would probably ask about some of his habits or appearances."

Scott suggests that parents try the same approach with their student. "Talk about what you're noticing and ask your child, 'Do a lot of people where you live have tattoos like that? Does the symbol on your ankle have a particular meaning?'

"Find out if it's common, in your son's community, to sleep during the day and stay up all night. As he sits in front of the computer for hours at a time playing video games, ask if his friends are all wired to their computers too, and find out how they communicate with each other if they're all wearing headphones."

Just as you would probably explain your culture and your family traditions to an exchange student, Scott says, you can remind your son or daughter of the way things are in your household.

"Tell them, 'Here at our house, we go to bed before midnight. You'll find it's a lot easier to sleep between eleven or twelve at night and seven in the morning, because that's when we sleep. And since everyone here helps with chores, we'd appreciate it if you would take care of the breakfast dishes sometime before noon so the kitchen will be clean when we make lunch.'"

College students are not slow-witted. They'll pick up on the sarcasm, but they'll also appreciate that you are asking about their appearance or reminding them of family routines rather than either accusing them of doing something wrong or stoically pretending that nothing has changed.

Students *do* change over the course of their college years. They are going through a process of confronting their past, present, and future. They are questioning themselves, testing new directions, doubting their abilities, and discovering impressive qualities in themselves. All young adults examine their self-image, and most will make at least some changes based on what they are learning about themselves.

Throughout their college years, but especially during the first year or two, students are asking questions that families find uncomfortable. As hard as it may be for you, this is work your child must do. Students are looking for the answers to the Five W's: Who, Where, What, When, and Why.

- **Who am I?** Students are engaged in the normal, but painful, process of separating the self from the family. During the college years, it is not unusual to try out behaviors and appearances and values that differ from those they were raised with. Questioning is part of the process of assimilation that must occur for their values to become their own.

- **Where do I belong?** College students start to think about how their family's social position and income influence them in new settings, and how these realities can affect their own position in the future.

- **What will I do with my life?** Students recognize that by the time they leave college, they will want a sense of what comes next. Some students come to college with a clear and unbending vision of their future, but most need to figure out what it means to apply their values through their work and actions.

- **When does it all begin?** When do I grow up? Students express a constant desire for whatever comes next—the next semester, next stage in a relationship, or the next phase of life. They are waiting for the moment when everything finally will feel complete, when people will consider them adults at last. That was supposed to happen when they got to college, but now they find that college is just more preparation.

- **Why?** The three-year-old's constant "why" re-emerges in college. Students will pick apart a relationship, a plan, or their past and analyze it almost to the point of obsession. This is part of the growth process, and it is connected to the fear of making a mistake with their newfound responsibilities. They are seeing old, familiar ideas in brand-new ways, which can be disquieting. They struggle with the idea that life is not just black and white, ideas are not just right or wrong, but that there are many shades of gray.

Each time your student comes home, and especially during the first year, you will need to figure out how to fit your family back together again. It can be a slow, grating challenge as you try out the old roles and realize they no longer seem comfortable. Then again, rather than experiencing a slow adjustment phase, you may run headfirst into a major collision with your newly independent child. More than one family has seen their student come home over spring break and in short order accuse his parents of hypocrisy.

"You send a check to the Sierra Club every year, and you claim to be such an environmentalist, so why do you have to drive that big SUV around town? You seem to think that everyone else in the world should conserve energy, but you get to pollute the whole valley."

As uncomfortable as it is to have your child challenge your beliefs and behaviors, your explanation is important to him. In this case, your student is probably not saying you should stop sending that check to the Sierra Club, nor should you get rid of the car. He probably likes driving it as much as you do, but he may genuinely want to know how you have managed to put these seemingly disparate behaviors together. Maybe you respond by admitting that you wanted a truck all your life, but you could never have one because you needed a family vehicle; your son might come to see that having this SUV is a way to quietly fulfill your long-held fantasy. Or you may acknowledge that you always worried about your children's safety in your previous car and in this one you feel that your family is more protected; this gives your son a glimpse of his parents' priorities. He still may disagree with your rationale, but it helps him to see how you reach your decisions.

You may feel that your child is rebelling against everything you ever taught her. Even though your child is questioning the way she was raised or the things you believe in most deeply, she has heard your lessons throughout her life, and she is taking your words into consideration. She will not completely reject out of hand everything she's ever learned.

As we campus staff members walk through residence halls, listen to class discussions, or overhear students in the cafeteria, we frequently hear them say, "My parents think . . ." or "My mom says . . ." or "In my family, we always. . . ." Students know their parents' opinions, and they care what their family thinks. The student who lights up her first cigarette is thinking, if not saying, "My dad would kill me if he knew I was smoking."

Every college student makes choices his parents would criticize. Nonetheless, you can trust that by the time your child reaches eighteen, he or she knows what you believe. Your words will pass through his mind as he makes his decisions. And even if family values drop out of sight for a while, they usually reappear by graduation.

WHO IS THIS KID, AND WHAT DID THEY DO WITH MY *REAL* CHILD?

When parents leave their students at college, one of their great fears is that their child will change *too* much. They expect their child to become more mature, to grow in intellect, to gain a focus on life. It can be hard, though, to think of all those changes happening when you are not around to watch the progress.

Throughout high school, Miguel had been cynical about athletics and most of the typical after-school organizations. He and his friends scorned the student council members and class officers; anything resembling school spirit irritated him. His own extracurricular activities revolved around drama club, debate, and the school play.

At college, though, his outlook changed dramatically. At his small liberal arts college, he joined the newspaper staff, volunteered to give tours for the admissions office, and signed up for training to become an orientation leader. As a sophomore he was elected to the student assembly, and the next year he ran for student body president. When his parents visited him on campus, he seemed to be admired by everyone, and he was obviously flourishing.

College can bring on a complete personality reversal. Miguel's parents were impressed with all the growth they saw in him, but they couldn't help but wish they had been a part of it. It almost felt as if they might have been the reason he was so cynical all those years; as soon as he moved away from home, he became energized and excited. It was not his family that made the difference, though. In the small-school atmosphere of Miguel's college campus—rather than the huge and highly programmed high school he had attended—he saw that his efforts could make a genuine difference.

Sometimes the changes go the other way. Students can get lost in the freedom of their new way of life. Instructors don't take attendance, and if students don't turn in a paper, no one asks for it. There are few rules, and with a bit of ingenuity, most of them can be broken. And every college student has lapses of judgment. Your daughter gives $100 to a stranger because he had a sad story; your son loses his backpack; your child leaves the apartment unlocked, and a computer is stolen.

The college years are a staging ground for adulthood. In most cases, mistakes are made within the relative safety of a supportive environment, and there are people around to help students pick up the pieces. Not every problem is easily remedied, though—the unplanned pregnancy, the run-in with the police after a night of drinking, or the inappropriate behavior that leads to a charge of sexual assault. For parents, news like this is devastating. This is not the way you raised your child, and it's hard to understand how such things could have happened.

When students make mistakes, their reaction may be to give up and drop out of school rather than work to find a solution. Parents, meanwhile feel the need to step in and fix the problem. Colleges routinely hear pleas from parents saying, "He's only a kid! Can't you let this go?" Whether it's underage drinking, plagiarism, or lighting a dumpster on fire after a basketball victory, there are families asking for leniency, just this once and just for their child.

People over the age of eighteen are adults who are responsible for their actions, and they must be prepared to face the consequences when they make mistakes. This is part of the maturing process. Colleges, like society, enact rules and policies in order to ensure a safe community for everyone who lives, works, and studies on campus.

When a student breaks the rules, family members have to decide if they can help—and realistically, whether they even *should* help. It may be the hardest thing you've ever done to tell your student you cannot intervene and you will not fix the mess he's in. It may also be the best thing you can do. When students think their parents will continue to protect them from the consequences of their behaviors, they do not feel a need to grow up and accept responsibility. Facing the outcome of a serious mistake is a painful process, but facing it is better than doing nothing—and much better than repeating the mistake.

Some eighteen to twenty-year-olds simply do not belong in college. If that sounds like your son or daughter, you will want to work with your child to think about what comes next. You don't have to, and should not, support a college education if your student is not going to take advantage of it. That does not mean, however, that your child is not "college material." Most colleges are willing to defer enrollment if a student decides to take a break for a semester or two. Advisers and counselors will often encourage a student who is having academic problems to take some time off. Work or travel experiences can help students identify interests or decide on a major. If a year off helps a student mature, focus, and develop a commitment to education, it's time well spent.

Nearly every student makes at least some changes during the

first two years of college. As the years pass, though, that stranger begins to look more and more familiar. The daughter who blasted her religious training ends up getting married in the church where she received her first communion or the syna-gogue where she had her bat mitzvah. The son who questioned his family's politics ends up voting for the same candidate as his father. Children call home to ask for their grandmother's holiday recipes, and eventually they want all those books, toys, and clothes they stuffed into the attic years ago.

However, the turnaround doesn't happen quickly, and it usu-ally doesn't yield a totally satisfying outcome. Your children will be different from you, just as you are different from your parents. You probably rejected some of your own parents' practices and values, and few parents are completely satisfied with all of their children's choices.

You're still going to enjoy watching them as they start their careers and move on with their lives. In the meantime, focus on the positive. Most parents, when they stop and think about the differences they've seen since their child started college, say that he or she is more independent and mature, more intelligent, and more appreciative of home and family.

QUICK TIPS FOR STUDENTS

- Before your parents come for the family weekend or before you go home for a visit, take a quick assessment: What has changed about you since the last time your family saw you? Do you look different? Are you dressing differently? Do you have new habits, or have you accepted a new core belief that your family is not expecting? Give them a call and let them know in advance. It's a challenge for parents when they're dishing up the Saturday night stew to hear their son announce, "I'm a vegetarian. I won't eat that stuff." An unexpected hair color or a tattoo can be a shock. You'll help your family adjust, and while you still may face some conflict, it's likely to be milder than if they had had no warning.

- Expect and respect new family patterns. *You* have changed since you left home; don't be surprised if your family has, too. If there's something that really bothers you, mention it, but don't consider their changes a personal insult. Look for the benefits and tell them when you notice something you like. They'll be amazed by your maturity.

- If you have a problem—you've overdrawn your checking account, someone stole your backpack, or you're failing chemistry—tell your parents. Remember when you were in high school and they told you, "If you get in trouble, I'd rather hear about it from you than from someone else"? They still feel that way. Now it's probably going to be your responsibility, not theirs, to fix the problem, so think through the issue, develop a plan, and then tell them both the problem and what you're doing to solve it.

- If there's a *big* problem, put yourself in their care. You don't need to come up with the perfect way to bring up the topic. Just say, "Mom, Dad, I need to tell you. . . ." (And it doesn't hurt to tell them "I'm scared.")

- Give your family the good news. Parents need to hear about your successes, and they are among the few who will truly, deeply share your pride.

- Just for fun, at least once a year, thank them for something they taught you, gave you, or inspired in you.

CHAPTER 10

Moving Out, Moving On

Leaving Dorm Life Behind

After Peg helped her son move into the residence hall at the beginning of his freshman year, she drove home feeling overwhelmed with pride. Willie, now a quiet and mature young man, was starting a new life at a prestigious East Coast university. They had talked about the challenges he would face, and he was determined he would succeed. Good grades and recommendations from professors would get him into a top medical school someday. Peg would be paying back college loans for years, but Willie had a bright future.

Six weeks later, she got a phone call early on a Saturday morning. Willie was yelling to be heard over the pounding bass of a boom box in the background. "Mom! Guess what! I just got invited to pledge a fraternity, and I'm moving into this big old house with forty-two of the greatest guys I ever met! This is the best!"

Today's college parents probably formed their opinions of fraternities and sororities many years ago. In the social conscience atmosphere of the late 1960s and 1970s, many college students concluded that fraternities and sororities were elitist and exclusive. Membership was a highly selective process, and more students were rejected than initiated. That reputation was both championed and challenged in the 1978 movie *Animal House,* and during the 1980s and 1990s, the popular image of fraternities declined into a picture of degeneration. As the 1990s drew to a close, many chapters were reduced to renting out rooms to non-members, just to keep their houses afloat. Hazing and the well-publicized outcomes of wild parties, including injuries and deaths related to heavy drinking, turned the tide against the so-called greek societies.

On a national level and on many local campuses, fraternities and sororities are fighting back. At their best, greek chapters are a tremendous asset to the campus and the community. Ideally, upperclassmen look out for new recruits, mentoring them through the first years of college. Philanthropy and campus involvement are requirements of membership, and greeks often take the lead on college events like homecoming and student elections, as well as community activities such as food drives, trash pickups, and tree planting. Members are expected to maintain good grades; the chapter elects an academic officer who ensures that students attend classes regularly, study diligently, and understand that graduation in good standing reflects well on the entire house.

At their worst, however, fraternities and sororities continue the *Animal House* saga. On some campuses, neglected fraternity houses have been condemned, chapters have been banned, or the entire greek system has been eliminated.

How do you, as a parent, differentiate between the good and the bad houses? How can you know if the fraternity or sorority your child wants to join will be a positive influence or a negative one?

When Tracie called home to tell her parents she had been invited to pledge a sorority, they were worried. "I've heard about the parties and the problems," her father said. "Tracie is saying this is a science and engineering house for women, and the girls who live there are good students. She says they'll help her when she has questions with classes like physics and calculus. But I'm not happy about the whole fraternity and sorority scene. It seems like trouble."

Parents can do their homework, researching the national organization's Web site by searching online for the name of the group. They also can check the college's Web site to see if additional information is available on the local chapter. A student affairs professional on campus should be able to tell you if the chapter has had recent problems, if it is on probation as a student group, or if it has a good reputation.

The best indicator of the character of the chapter that is recruiting your child, however, is your own student. Greek houses are small communities; members decide whom they will invite to pledge, and they want to maintain the environment they have created. Fraternities and sororities have a good idea, when they ask new pledges to join, that the student will fit into their house's culture. If your son or daughter is a conscientious student who speaks out for social justice issues, he or she is not likely to be invited to join a group that spends Monday through Wednesday recovering from weekend binges.

Commuter students don't often think about joining a fraternity or sorority, but belonging to a chapter can address many of the college problems they typically face. Membership often does not require living in the house, but commuters who pledge find they have a houseful of supportive friends, along with a place in which to study between classes, to eat, and to socialize. And the commuter who decides to move closer to campus has a room waiting.

Fraternity and sorority houses can be viewed as an extension of the college residence hall. As in the dorm, students live together in a close community; the difference is that they select their own membership, and they regard each other more as family than as housemates. They choose new members each year who, they believe, are at least in some ways like themselves and who share common values. They want to feel that they can come back in five or ten years and still feel at home with their "brothers" or "sisters."

This call for comfort—wanting to be with a caring and supportive group of friends—is a natural response to the upheaval of college life. Students might choose a large university because of all the possibilities it offers, but they still want to go home at night to a safe and familiar spot with "people like me."

At the same time, though, college should be a time to learn about diversity and difference. Any number of campus programs will be available to expand students beyond their comfort zone in a carefully constructed learning atmosphere. Even if your daughter chooses the safety of a sorority, she should strike out to experience some of the new and different adventures that college offers.

"2 BDRM, OFF-ST PKG, NR UNIV"

At some point, you can expect your child to announce: "My friends and I are going to get an apartment. We looked at some places that are just a couple blocks from campus, and it's going to be way less expensive than the residence halls. I just thought I'd let you know. Okay?"

Sometimes the message is a bit more ominous:

"I missed the housing reapplication deadline for next year, so I don't have any place to live. There's a guy in my math class who needs a roommate for fall semester, though. I think I'll take a look at his place."

"I absolutely cannot stand my roommate another week! I'm

moving out of the dorm and getting an apartment. I've looked through the want ads, and I'm going to check out some places this afternoon."

For commuter students, the announcement is accompanied by a calculation of the hours they can save by living closer to campus, the money they will save in gas or bus fares, and the academic benefits of living closer to campus.

Typically, parents first hear about an apartment midway through the freshman or sophomore year—long before they are ready for it. Parents feel safe when their student is living in a residence hall or at home. They believe their student already has sufficient independence, but guidance is comfortably nearby. In the residence hall, their child is setting his own hours, working out lifestyle decisions with roommates and neighbors, and making his own choices about what he will eat or how much he will study. At home, curfew rules and chore assignments have been relaxed to accommodate the commuter. How much more independence does he need?

Thinking about an apartment, parents once again revert to worrying about safety and their child's ability to take care of herself. They question the financial benefits, and the issue becomes all the more complicated when lease confirmation requires first and last months' rent plus a damage deposit. Your child is hoping you will hand over hundreds of dollars that were not in your budget, and your reaction is "If you think you're responsible enough to have an apartment, maybe you should be responsible enough to come up with the money yourself."

From a developmental standpoint, apartment living is an important step in learning to share responsibilities, identify priorities, and resolve conflicts with others in a relatively safe environment. These are all skills that will transfer to intimate relationships, marriage, and the world of work. The presence of roommates who are also college students continues the security and supportive atmosphere from the residence halls; young adults can work through life's difficulties in partnership with friends who are going through the same experiences and life stages.

An apartment represents independence, but not every student will be ready for an apartment when he starts his sophomore year, or for that matter, when he begins his junior year. The steps from dependence to responsibility are predictable, but they don't always fall in a straight line. If this is the first you've heard about an apartment, you may have cause for worry. Moving into an apartment should not be a snap decision. Peer pressure can cause students to link up with roommates they don't know well: "Everyone's getting apartments for next year. I don't want to be the only junior living in the dorm. I need to find three people to move in with. I'm just not sure yet who to ask."

It's not quite enough for you that your son or daughter is convinced everything will work out. You want to feel comfortable about this decision too. There are some obvious clues to indicate whether or not your child is ready for an apartment:

- *During the past year, has your child made good choices?* Are you confident that she can manage her finances? Are you comfortable with the friends she has made? Can she balance social, personal, and academic demands? Apartment living adds a whole new list of duties to a student's schedule for cooking, cleaning, and commuting. Time management skills are important.
- *Ask your child why he wants to live off campus. Are you satisfied by his answers?* Most students say they can save money by living off campus. Rent costs may sound less expensive than room and board in the residence hall, but be sure he has considered groceries, transportation costs, utilities, and parking. Are his estimates reasonable? In most college communities, on- and off-campus expenses tend to be comparable, but an apartment

might mean a twelve-month commitment. Students who say they will study better in an apartment, or they can't bear the noise or the food in the dorm for another year, might be surprised to find that life is no better in an apartment. If, however, your child says he is ready for an apartment, he wants the responsibility of his own place, and he recognizes that he will be taking care of himself, he is ready for the next step in the growing-up process.

Although even the best preparation cannot prevent every problem, it will help to discuss apartment issues long before your student is ready to sign a lease. During holiday or summer breaks, parents should be talking with their child about general guidelines for apartment life. Maybe you don't want your daughter living on the ground floor in a building with no security entrance; perhaps you want your son to live within walking distance of campus because he will not have a car. And you can ask your child to fix some meals and clean the bathroom at home as reassurance that he has the life skills necessary for apartment living.

If you still find yourself worrying about your student's leaving the protection of the residence hall, think about what your underlying concerns might be and whether they are realistic:

- *It's too much responsibility. She won't have time to study.* If your child has made an effort to develop good study habits, she will probably maintain them.
- *She won't eat well. She'll get sick.* Let her know this is a concern, and ask what she and her roommates plan to do about meals. You *should* be concerned if she says, "There's a taco joint right next door. We figure we'll eat there every day." On the other hand, you can stop worrying if she says she will sign up for a once-a-day meal plan at the dining center, or if she has a food service job lined up so that she can eat some meals on cam-

pus. If your student has done some thoughtful planning about food, and if she knows how to cook, she will be fine.

- *I'm worried about sex. I think he's getting an apartment so he can have his girlfriend over.* If students want to have sex, they will. An apartment might provide more privacy, but living arrangements are not the deciding factor in whether or not students have sex.

- *I've heard about the house parties near campus. I don't want to pay all that money for an apartment just so he can have drinking parties every weekend.* As with the sex issue, students who want to party will find a way. It's true that most students will occasionally want to host a party. At least some of the charm of having an apartment is being able to entertain friends, but in most cases, students are not going to risk their damage deposit or invite the possibility of eviction by throwing wild parties. You *should* be concerned if your child rents an apartment that has earned a recurring reputation for parties. The apartment building across the street from the football stadium or the rundown house in the block behind fraternity row might be a poor choice. If you know that your child routinely drinks too much on weekends, and he decides to rent a place that already reeks of stale beer, this apartment will not help him become a better scholar.

Renting an apartment is a significant step, and many parents still prefer to review the lease or even check the apartment before the student signs anything. Seeing the apartment is not always a possibility, especially for out-of-town parents, but the more you know about the lease, the apartment, and the roommates, the more comfortable you will feel.

A point to keep in mind, though: When you consider that an apartment usually combines two to five roommates, the "helpful advice" of anywhere from four to ten parents is completely over-whelming.

FRIENDS, ROOMMATES, OR LOVERS?

"One male or female roommate wanted, nonsmoker, to share two-bedroom apartment near campus."

You remember being twenty years old, and you know that young adults are thinking about sex. It's no wonder you panic when your child announces "Ted, Sally, and I found this great place to live next year."

Mixing sexes in an apartment still feels inappropriate to parents. How can college-age students *not* become intimately involved when they're living together? Even the most platonic intentions are too easily set aside when twenty-year-olds share a bathroom and sleep in adjoining rooms.

The questions are these: What will the relationship be? And are you—the parents—comfortable with this arrangement? As long as you're paying the rent, you can set a few limits, and many parents insist that their student live with others of the same sex.

Still, it can work well to have men and women share an apartment, as long as they approach the arrangement with a sense of reality and friendship. After students have spent freshman year in a mixed-sex residence hall, where students shuffle down to breakfast together wearing baggy sweatpants and slippers, without benefit of makeup or a shower, it's really not a big step to a nonsexual relationship in adjacent bedrooms in an apartment. When they select their first apartment mates, students usually pick friends, not lovers.

Moving in with a boyfriend or girlfriend is a decision that most students approach very cautiously. Living together represents a commitment. Students know that a breakup can leave them with serious and difficult choices about whom to turn to and where to live. While students might select roommates in a relatively nonchalant manner, figuring that the arrangement is only for a year, they don't savor the prospect of living with a former lover if the relationship goes bad.

APARTMENTS: THE GOOD, THE BAD, AND THE REALLY UGLY

The standards of student apartments vary immensely, ranging from old houses that have seen decades of use and abuse by college students to luxury high-rise apartments with built-in washers and dryers, separate bedroom-bath suites for each roommate, and a concierge in the lobby. Wherever students choose to live, they want to mark their new territory as their own. By decorating, deciding where to place their belongings, and establishing a routine in this new setting, they make it a home. Parents tread carefully when they venture into their child's first apartment. Do you ignore the obvious problems, or make the obvious suggestions?

Rose refused all offers of help when she moved into her first apartment, saying that she didn't want her mother to see the place until she and her roommate were settled in. Two weeks later, she called and invited her mother to come for dinner. "I can't wait for you to see what we've done! We hung some pictures and bought some plants. And I made new curtains for the kitchen. It's great. You'll love it."

As hard as her mother tried to focus on the decorating, though, she couldn't ignore the stained sofa in the living room, the dangling light fixture in the hallway, and the constant drip of the kitchen faucet. "You've done a wonderful job here," she told Rose midway through dinner. "The curtains look great, and the plants are a nice touch. I think, though, that the landlord needs to hear about that faucet and the hall light. And can you find out if he can replace the sofa, or at least pay for a cover for it? It's pretty bad."

"No, Mom, we don't dare complain! Do you know how lucky we were to get a place this close to campus? We want to live here next year, too, so we can't have the landlord thinking that we're troublemakers."

Students learn valuable lessons by living on their own, including what rights they have and how to get things done. Many young men and women have never had to solve problems or assert their rights without assistance from a parent, coach, or teacher, and they may not be prepared for the unexpected events that are sure to come up. One student called her father late at night, nearly hysterical: "Dad, there's a mouse in our apartment! What are we supposed to do? This is gross! A mouse. I can't stand it!"

"Laurel, it's not the end of the world," he told her. "No, you don't want mice in your apartment, but it's not going to actually hurt you. In the morning, you can call the apartment manager. They'll give you a trap or some poison to put out. And the important thing is that you probably need to clean your apartment. You usually get mice because there's something for them to eat. Sweep the floor, vacuum the carpet, and check the cupboards for any open food or boxes of food that a mouse could get into. And don't worry. It happens."

The concerns you felt when your child first announced plans to move into an apartment—that she was not ready for this step, that it was too much of a commitment—may continue throughout her first year of off-campus living. Most students will face at least a few problems as they learn to deal with the world of leases, landlords, and independent living. They will still want their parents' advice and the occasional practical help, though. "I bought an entertainment center. It was a real bargain, but I just realized, I don't have any tools. Can you come up this weekend and help me put it together?"

Your time—and any duplicate cookware, wrenches, or patio furniture you might have lying around—will be happily received. Your son or daughter will be grateful for a gift box of packaged foods in the mail or the occasional bag of groceries or containers of reheatable meals when you come to visit.

A twelve-month apartment lease most likely means your child will not come home for the summer. Although most students go home for the summer following the freshman year, the amount of time at home tapers off after the sophomore year, and the majority of students stay near campus or find work somewhere else after their junior year. By the time students move into their own apartment, they no longer have any doubts that college is their home. Even if you live only a twenty-minute drive away, and even if your student is in your laundry room every weekend washing and ironing clothes, having an apartment means he has moved out. Your child still needs you! Just not as much, and not in the same ways.

QUICK TIPS FOR STUDENTS

- If you go through fraternity or sorority rush, be yourself. Greek chapters are looking for pledges who will fit into their culture. If they don't see the real you, you could be setting yourself up for a miserable match.
- Joining a fraternity, sorority, or any other group should not require you to do anything to endanger yourself. If you are asked to drink excessively or perform any acts that feel uncomfortable in order to become a member of any organization, decline. You can find better friends.
- Moving into an apartment is a natural progression from resi-

dence hall living, but it calls for more responsibility. Do some solid research before committing yourself to a lease, and be sure you know what is included in the rent and what extra expenses you will have to pay. Are water, heat, and electricity provided? What about phone rates and computer hookups? Cable TV? How will you get from your apartment to campus? If you will need a car, will you have a parking space? Does parking cost extra?

- Consider the upfront costs of an apartment. If you must pay first and last months' rent and a damage deposit in order to confirm the lease, do you have that lump sum on hand? Do all roommates have their share of the deposits?

- If anything seems unclear about the arrangements you're making, the apartment you're planning to take, or the terms of the lease, ask for time to think it over. You should be able to see the exact apartment you will be renting, and the lease should stipulate the rental amount for the entire amount of the contract. Be cautious if there are stipulations for the rent to be raised at the discretion of the manager. In some leases, a single noise complaint could increase your rent or even be grounds for eviction.

- Talk with your roommates about how you will handle bill paying, how you will divide up household chores, and how you will deal with disagreements.

- Practice your housekeeping skills. Make sure you know how to cook, clean, and take care of minor household repairs. Hint: Your parents will be much more receptive to the idea of an apartment if you offer to do these tasks at home long before you suggest moving out of the dorm.

CHAPTER 11

What Can You Do with a Sociology Degree?

Choosing a Life, Not a Job

Every now and then, you notice someone who is obviously enjoying his work—the gardener at the botanical gardens, the chef at a sushi bar—and you think "I'd like that job. It looks like fun."

Students face these temptations every day. Colleges spread out a smorgasbord of academic appetizers and invite students to sample a little of everything. Liberal arts programs are set up so that students take courses in a range of subjects, giving them a basic understanding of the physical sciences, humanities, and social sciences. With each class they take, they are making judgments, deciding they want to delve deeper into one subject, or vowing they will never take a second course in another.

The developmental processes of young adults are also part of the mix. College students are at an age when they are reviewing and questioning all their belief systems, and the college curriculum is set up to encourage investigation, not only of new academic subjects but also of themselves. One of the most exciting outcomes of a good class schedule is the occasional "Eureka!" that happens when everything comes together. The book a student is reading for an English class portrays the same event as a painting in the art history textbook, and it all ties into this week's lecture in "Psychology of Religion" and Grandma's stories about her childhood in Georgia.

Parents send their student to college for an education, and they hope he will genuinely enjoy the process of learning, but the ultimate proof of a successful college career is not how he feels about all his classes. When their child walks off stage on graduation day, parents will want to know that he has a job waiting for him, he will earn a livable wage, and he has a comfortable future. They hope he will have health insurance coverage. They will cut him some slack only if he's going to graduate school to qualify for an even bigger salary and a more comfortable life in a couple of years.

THE NEW SCHOOLS OF THOUGHT

Colleges and universities have changed over time, and their role in career preparation continues to evolve. A century ago, the goal of universities was to turn out "educated citizens" who could read Latin and Greek, had studied certain critical works, and could converse intelligently. Most went on to become physicians, lawyers, politicians, or professors, but the overarching goal for university students was to learn a body of knowledge that would provide an educated view of the world.

Even thirty or forty years ago, the fact that a student earned a college degree was proof of potential, but it did not necessarily provide entry to a specific career. Technical colleges and business schools were the path for those who wanted to learn a trade or skill, but colleges and universities taught students "how to learn." When they arrived at college as freshmen, the major question students needed to answer was whether they were headed toward a degree in the sciences or one in the arts. A liberal arts graduate could count on getting a job somewhere—anywhere—then she could work her way up in the profession. A student who majored in psychology might qualify for an entry-level position in social work, marketing, or business and advance from there. An English degree could lead to journalism, library work, grant writing, or a business career.

In the 1980s and 1990s, though, growing numbers of students began to look to universities for preparation in a specific job, not for a general education. They questioned the need for courses outside their field of study and challenged the notion that they needed a broad educational background. A student might take every computer course the school offered and then leave without graduating, thinking, "I can get the job I want with what I know right now. Why take a bunch of classes to learn things I'll never need? I'm better off earning a paycheck."

Today, students, parents, and employers are seeing the value of combining career preparation with a liberal education as a long-term strategy for an ever-changing economy. Every job posting seems to require good communication skills, and students have come to appreciate the importance of what they are learning in speech and writing classes. They can increase their value to an employer and their chances for international work if they know a second or third language and if they can discuss with some competence what they learned in cultural studies.

THE CHANGING MIND

Most students start college with a career focus. In order to get through the day, the week, and the semester, students operate under the assumption that they have a plan in mind—a major that will lead to a career that will, in turn, lead to a lifetime of fulfillment, wealth, and happiness. They don't dwell on those long-term goals every day, but knowing they have a destination keeps them on track.

As students explore a range of college subjects, however,

career goals can change—sometimes for the most unexpected reasons. A student might take a course because it's required, but finds it's the only subject they really makes sense to him: "I like the way philosophy majors think. That constant questioning, looking for the logic and the deeper meaning—it's fun to be challenged like that."

An instructor who loves his subject can bring a lecture to life and draw a student into a field of study. Matt, who was "kind of thinking about a psych major," signed up for geology because it was the only four-credit lab class that fit his second-semester schedule. Although much of the textbook for the course centered on rock identification and plate tectonics, Matt was fascinated by the stories the professor told during class. "This guy can make *rocks* exciting! The day he talked about coral reefs—how changes in rock temperature and water currents can affect the reefs—I was actually disappointed when the lecture ended. I could have listened to him for hours. I would *love* to know a subject as well as he does."

The next year, Matt took another class from the same professor, and the following summer, he applied for a job in the geology lab. Eventually, he decided to go to graduate school to study hydrogeology, a subject he never knew existed before he started college.

Sometimes students come face-to-face with the reality that they picked the wrong major. If students find that they are bored or disillusioned by the classes in their major, they face a tremendous letdown. Worse, they may find they do not qualify for the major they dreamed of. The student who planned to be veterinarian will be forced to rethink his goals if he can't pass organic chemistry.

The most common reason for switching majors, though, is that students change. The careful, conservative sophomore who settled on a "safe" choice when he started college now recognizes that he has great potential and does not need to limit himself. His wild-eyed, unfocused roommate discovers his passion and becomes centered. Education at its best opens students to new possibilities and encourages them to dare to expand their choices.

The student who is re-examining career goals has a lot to think about and is probably agonizing over her decisions. Aside from the philosophical issues, there are some purely practical considerations: A few, or perhaps even all, of the classes she has taken may not count toward a new major. Some students must essentially start over or transfer to another university that offers the degree they want.

And there is the fear of disappointing parents. Every year college counselors hear students say, "I wish I could change my major, but I can't do that to my family. They had their hearts set on me becoming a doctor" (or majoring in law, being an engineer, or taking over the family business).

Often parents truly are disappointed. You expect your child to refine and refocus her life plans during college. A change from art history to graphic arts may seem like a smart, strategic move, but it is much harder to understand where your child is headed when she switches from business administration to gender studies. A father complains that his son wants to switch from the engineering department to education. "He hasn't really thought this through! I think he's just listening to his friends. They're all English and history majors, and they don't have much respect for science and engineering. But I don't think my son realizes how much less he would earn as a teacher. I'm afraid he's throwing away his future."

As a parent, you can hardly help but ask questions: Are you sure? When did you make this decision? Have you talked to anyone about this? *Why?*

If your child decides to change majors, he may face an additional year of college, which can cost $10,000 to $30,000 or more, depending on the school. At some point, you and your child may need to talk about the consequences of changing direction, but part of the discussion should include weighing the financial costs against a few years—or a lifetime—of being stuck in the wrong career.

THE PLANNING PROCESS

Career planning and selection is a four-year, four-step process, and it doesn't pay to take shortcuts. In order for students to find a satisfying career match, they need to give careful thought and attention to each of the steps. Think of career planning as a series of MILEstones on the career path:

M Matching: personal values and interests fitting with potential professions.

I Information gathering: determining the skills and knowledge needed for a field of study and acquiring an education.

L Limiting the options: assessing the range of jobs within a professional field and focusing on a specific career.

E Employment qualification: gaining practical experience in the field and mastering the job application process.

M—The Matching Step

This step ties in with the self-exploration that students are naturally engaged in during their first year or two of college. As they are identifying their personal values, interests, skills, and abilities, they are developing the very information they need to know in order to lay the foundation for their career. What kind of a lifestyle do they want? What personal talents and abilities can they draw on? Do they prefer a daily routine, or do they need constant challenge and stimulation? And how do the answers to these questions match with the career options they are considering?

Whether or not students are ready to identify a career, most young adults have some sense of how they want to spend their lives—they just don't yet have much experience in expressing their vision of the future. A college career adviser can help students think about and describe the kind of life they want to lead.

"Let's take a look at yourself five years from now," the adviser might say. "It's a Monday morning, and you're waking up, getting ready for work. Don't think too much about the details of your job, but imagine what your life will be like.

"Are you living in an apartment? A house? If you look out the window by your bed, what do you see? Are you in a city? In the country? Is it *this* country?

"What clothes are you putting on for work? Jeans and T-shirt? Casual dress? A business suit? A uniform? What kind of shoes are you putting on?

"You head out the door to go to work. Do you get into a car and drive? Do you catch a bus? Walk? Ride a bike?

"What does your workplace look like when you get there? Are you in a big city, a small city, or a rural area? Do you work in an office building? A lab? Maybe you'll be working outside all day?

"If you have clients or customers, what are they like? What are *they* wearing?"

As students think about the way they want to live, they will begin to see that some professions will support that lifestyle, and others will not.

Career advisers can also administer a number of standard tests that help students understand their personality traits and consider how those characteristics relate to specific professions. An introvert probably won't be happy in a position that requires him to meet the public all day, every day. Someone who relies on careful planning will not want to work in a job with constant surprises. Similarly, the career adviser can help students identify how their natural skills and abilities might apply to different careers, further clarifying job options.

As a parent, you can help by encouraging your child to talk to a career adviser on campus at least once during the freshman and sophomore years, and to check in more frequently during the junior and senior years. You can also help your student identify personal qualities and potential careers by having her think about which extracurricular activities she most enjoys, which classes seem most interesting, what kinds of homework she spends the most time on, and which professors seem most engaging. You can talk about your perception of the ways she works best, or how others seem to relate to her. You may have noticed that she is the person all her friends come to when they have problems, or you may believe that she seems happiest when she's working alone. Her high school teachers may all have reported that she became frustrated when she was asked to complete an assignment during class on a short deadline, but she turned in excellent work when she had enough time to rewrite or check her answers.

Discussions of such observations require great care. It is an understatement to say that students don't always take personal comments well from their parents. The goal is not to criticize or point out shortcomings, but to identify characteristics as strengths. It is not wrong to work slowly or to prefer solitude; there are careers where those characteristics are an asset.

I—The Information-Gathering Step

In this step, students are looking at what they must do, what they must learn, and how long it will take to qualify for the professions they are considering. The student who wants to become a lawyer will have to determine if he will be able to handle the demands of the course work, if he has the finances to pay for law school, and if he is willing to devote the time to more education after completing his undergraduate degree. The potential concert violinist must face the daunting question of whether she has the talent and perseverance to prepare for such a competitive field.

During this phase of the career investigation process, students can find strong support on campus. An academic counselor will help define the departmental major and educational requirements for the professions students are considering. The faculty adviser can discuss the pros and cons of a graduate degree and connect students with instructors who teach in the field for more information.

Students should also be working with their career advising office. In some cases, a career adviser can identify several different academic programs that will lead to the same career. The student who is interested in a corporate career might believe that the college's business program is the only option. However, depending on the kind of job she ultimately wants, she might be better prepared by studying economics in the liberal arts department, marketing in the communications department, or agricultural business in the agriculture department.

In addition, career advisers can help students set up informational interviews with people working in the field who can talk about the real-world experience of the job. The more students know about the career, the better they will be able to understand and prepare for it.

By the end of their second year of college, students should have some sense of a general career area that most interests them and be ready to declare a major. This is a significant step for students, but it can lead to disappointment for parents who had their own ideas about their child's future profession. When you hear that your son is majoring in sociology, you can't imagine how he will ever get a job. Your daughter announces she has decided on Russian history, and you cannot fathom a career path.

Parents, like their student, need to keep an open mind about the possibilities and continue to go through the stages one step at a time. Sociology majors find jobs in business, human services, criminal justice, social work, and government. A history degree can lead to museum work, diplomatic service, and journalism jobs.

L—The Limiting Step

During the junior and senior years, students will be increasingly immersed in their area of study. They begin to see a subject in depth, and they learn to apply their knowledge and expand their understanding of the major. In these contexts, career options become increasingly clear.

Any academic major is made up of a variety of specialties. A student who decides to study English in order to become a playwright signs up for a Shakespeare course so that he can study some of the best plays of all time. The student sitting next to him is an English major because she loves to analyze symbolism in literature.

In the limiting step, students begin to understand the intricacies of a field of study and narrow their focus to the specialty that most interests them. The choices students make at this phase help them see their future more clearly. The architecture student decides that she prefers renovating historic buildings rather than designing new ones; the future math teacher hopes he can teach geometry at the high school level.

Some students might still be trying to identify a career; they have two or more options in mind, and they are not ready to give up either one. "I really like biology, but I think I might want to be a lawyer someday. Most pre-law students get a degree in political science, so maybe I should change my major."

Not only might a minor or a second major be the answer to combining multiple interests into a satisfying career, but it also can provide a way to distinguish a student from all the others in his class. The aspiring attorney learns that a biology degree with a political science minor is the best possible preparation for a future in environmental law. Similarly, a journalism student decides to get a second major in religious studies so that she can become a religion reporter.

An adviser in the college career center can help students find a mentor in the fields they're considering. Mentors have insights into what skills are currently needed or are likely to be valuable in the near future. Students need to keep up with emerging changes in their field to see the full range of possibilities, and they can get their best information from a mentor, a personable instructor, or a career services adviser who knows the kinds of jobs recent graduates have taken.

Students can also learn the newest trends in their field by joining a student organization related to their academic major. Student groups frequently invite professionals to come to campus to talk about current issues in the profession.

Parents can help in this stage by encouraging students to take advantage of the full range of career exploration opportunities available to them, and to take note of the people they're meeting. Regina, a communications major, always carried a small notebook with her and wrote down the names of guest lecturers in her courses, speakers who addressed the Communication Club, and everyone she met when she toured her mentor's workplace. When the time came to look for an internship, she sent notes to every person she had listed in her notebook, asking for advice. "I'm sure some of them wondered, 'Who is this person and why is she writing to me?'" she said. "But it worked. I actually got two internships—a semester-long internship at a news bureau in

Dallas, and a summer position working at the Democratic National Convention."

E—The Employment Step

This stage encompasses the serious work of getting an internship and a job. It starts with developing skills for the job hunt and continues through the process of landing a position. It includes preparing a résumé, writing cover letters, making follow-up phone calls, and interviewing first for internships, then for a professional position.

If students wait until graduation to begin their job search, they will have lost valuable time. A typical entry-level job posting is likely to look something like this:

> **Help wanted**   Public relations firm seeks graphic designer with proven track record in design and layout of printed materials. BA from accredited college or university, and two years' experience.

This is the Catch-22 of the job market: You can't get a job without experience, and you can't get experience without a job.

The answer to the problem is internships, those short-term positions that give students a chance to put their classroom skills into practice under the supervision of a practicing professional. Internships have become almost a requirement for upperclassmen, particularly in majors such as journalism, marketing, and business. The "demonstrated knowledge" or "previous experience" that employers demand as preparation for an entry-level position must come from somewhere, and students are putting multiple internships together to meet the requirements.

Students struggle to fit yet another obligation into their schedule, and it's especially challenging when the internship is unpaid and must be squeezed in among class, study, and paid employment hours: "I have to have a car to get to my intern job, but having a car means I need money for insurance and gas. Since the internship doesn't pay anything, I guess I have to keep waiting tables."

As internships have become a necessary step in career preparation, they have become increasingly competitive. Landing an internship—even an unpaid position—with a Fortune 500 company seems like a coup. When it comes time to apply for a professional position, however, students will need to be able to document what they learned in their internship. A three-month stint of performing menial tasks—such as filing or running errands—even if it is at a major firm, is less useful in the long run than a position at a less prestigious company where the student was able to build a Web site or be part of the development team that created a five-year marketing plan.

Parents can be helpful in the internship search by encouraging their student to consider in advance what the outcomes are likely to be:

- What tasks will the student be doing?
- What will the student learn?
- Does the internship provide credits toward graduation? Some internships allow students to earn academic credits through a career exploration course.
- Is there a chance that an unpaid internship might lead to a paid internship?
- How will this position help toward qualifying for a job in the future? Is that future job the one that the student really wants?

Internships are usually scheduled during the junior year, the summer before or after the junior year, or early in the senior year, but they can come earlier or later.

By the first semester of the senior year, then, students should be starting their search for a post-graduate job. Students should be checking with their campus career service office for the dates of upcoming workshops and job fairs. Résumé-writing workshops will help produce a polished résumé for the professional world, and a career adviser can critique application materials and cover letters. Interview workshops will provide tips and experience in interviewing. Students can also go back to the professionals who served as their mentors or internship supervisors to ask for job-seeking advice.

When recruiters come to campus, students in business, engineering, or other technical fields might find themselves much in demand, while liberal arts majors become convinced that the job hunt is hopeless. Although students have heard for years that their liberal arts background is the best possible training for a well-rounded employee, they grow discouraged as they look at job notices that ask for specialized training or technical skills— qualifications they do not have.

Liberal arts students *are* well qualified for a number of jobs, but they have to work harder to get a job offer. Campus job fairs might not be the answer, and it will take more time and energy to check multiple job sources, study the position listings, and work to convince employers that they are the right person for the job.

Newspaper want ads list only a small percentage of available positions. Online listings and campus job boards will be more helpful, especially for liberal arts majors. And networking works. The internship supervisor who knows that a student is looking for a job can ask his colleagues about openings and provide a reliable reference at the same time.

BUILDING RÉSUMÉS AND PORTFOLIOS

Candidates for internships and professional positions know they must have a résumé, but for college students seeking jobs today, an electronic résumé, or "portfolio," is becoming the new standard. A one- or two-sheet list of accomplishments and references is a starting point, but in order to compete for the top jobs, students are realizing that it helps to "show, not tell."

By linking to a personal Web site or burning a CD, students can show prospective employers proof of their accomplishments. A writing sample can be posted onto a Web site; a short video clip will demonstrate presentation skills as well as computer mastery; a link to the academic transcript will provide grade information; a slide presentation can track a community service project from start to finish.

The problem students face in creating a résumé or an electronic portfolio is that they must create one when they're least likely to have any spare time. If the deadline for graduate school applications is two weeks away, they may not have time to write an essay, gather recommendations from professors, and put together a résumé. When they find out that the campus job fair is this week, they will have to buy a suit, practice interviewing, and quickly put together a portfolio. In the frenzy, they can barely remember what they did last month, let alone recall their service learning experience from the previous semester or come up with an explanation of how their summer job served as a step in their career development.

College students accomplish amazing achievements through their volunteer and organizational efforts, as well as through work experience. A volunteer for Habitat for Humanity joins forces with members of the community to rehabilitate a home, and gains experience not only in carpentry, plumbing, laying carpet, and grouting tile, but also in team building and conflict resolution. A sorority organizes a food drive and stocks the community food shelf for a month, and members learn about event planning and customer service. Six students recognize that community college transfer students need extra support when they arrive at the university, so they draft bylaws and establish a new campus organization. In the process, they learn about organizational structure and meeting management.

Unfortunately, students seldom recognize the life and career skills they pick up from their club activities and community service. Fund-raising, record keeping, membership recruitment, and problem solving are all skills that future employers are seeking. By the time students are ready to graduate, though, they have forgotten the activities they participated in as freshmen, and they fail to see the progress they've made over their college career. Even as a freshman, it makes sense for a student to set aside a bit of time each semester to document her involvement in activities and her accomplishments. A résumé for an internship or for a professional position after college should be not just a list of memberships and jobs, but also evidence of how the student contributed to the group or the position and the skills that he or she has developed.

Parents can help by encouraging their student to work on career planning and résumé development throughout college, even if she has not yet selected an academic major. Many of the skills that students acquire, both in and out of the classroom, are likely to apply to many careers. Your child may take a job as a ski instructor because it's a good way to get a little money plus free ski time, but she may not recognize that teaching develops patience, the ability to work with a wide range of ages, and leadership experience.

MY PARENTS SPENT $80,000 ON COLLEGE, AND ALL I GOT WAS THIS CLERICAL JOB

Students start out their college career thinking they are on the fast track to a high-paying job. Nearly half of all students believe they will be top management within five years, and more than 80 percent think they will meet their career goals in ten years.[23] We've all heard of the business administration grad who stepped from college into a $75,000-a-year job, or the computer engineer who was snapped up a week after graduation for a six-figure income. We've also all heard of the more typical scenarios—the political science graduate who is working for a roofing company, and the geography major who manages a coffee shop.

Slowly, students catch on that their first job after graduation is not likely to provide the dream lifestyle they were expecting, at least not right away. They know they'll feel better when they have a job lined up, but they have not given much thought to how long they will need to stay in a job in order to prepare for a next step. They think they must apply only for the best-paying jobs or that they should jump right into graduate school in order to qualify for a better position in two or three years.

Parents, advisers, and faculty frequently have a better long-term view than the student when it comes to developing career strategies. Students are relieved when parents or advisers suggest that working for a nonprofit organization will be good training for a better-paying opportunity in a corporation in a year or two. Or it makes sense when a professor recommends a couple of years working in the field as good preparation for graduate school.

Nevertheless, the future doesn't always present itself on a prescribed schedule. For a large percentage of students, commencement day brings conflicting emotions—they're done with college, but they have nothing entered on their PDA for tomorrow.

Neither the student nor his parents should worry too much if that first professional job is not secured by graduation. Waiting tables or mowing lawns is not the worst option for students during the summer after graduation. A job applicant needs to have some money coming in, but he also needs flexibility for scheduling interviews. The credentials are in hand, and a job will come with persistence. Positions *do* open up throughout the summer and on into fall, and students might be better off starting the job search once the degree is in hand.

In the meantime, it feels good to spend at least a few months living in the present rather than focusing on the future. As Mei pointed out shortly after she graduated, "High school was all about preparing for college, and college was preparation for a career. Now my mother thinks I should find a job that will pay enough so I can afford my own apartment and a car. After that, she'll want me to start looking for a husband so that I can get married and have babies. She's got me on some fast-track schedule, but I really would like to have time to enjoy this stage of my life—being young, not having major responsibilities yet. What I'd really like to do is go to London, work in a pub for six months, and then come back and look for a job related to my major."

Temporary or part-time positions may not be what you and your child planned for post-college life, but they can lead to career-path jobs. Teaching an exercise course at the YMCA, doing research for a professor's grant project, or raising funds for an election campaign provide transferable skills. The Peace Corps, AmeriCorps, and Teach for America are exciting transition options, giving students experience as well as opportunities to focus on career directions. As an added bonus, some of these volunteer positions can reduce the amount students must repay on their student loans.

Staying in the college community for anywhere from a few months to a couple of years is typical. For students who are still trying to establish career credentials, lining up a summer internship near campus after graduation might improve the résumé and give them the credentials they need for a professional position. Campus career offices host recruiters and post job listings year-round, and at most colleges, alumni can continue to use the career office after graduation. The chance meeting with a professor or a suggestion from a career adviser can supplement the job hunt and boost the student's ego.

Whether or not there's a job waiting as soon as your student steps off the stage at graduation, you're both headed for yet another transition.

QUICK TIPS FOR STUDENTS

- You will change a lot during your college years. Don't feel that you have to stick to the career goal you declared as a first-term freshman. If one of your classes seems especially interesting, or if you meet someone with an intriguing job, allow yourself to think about how you might like a career in that area.
- While you're keeping your mind open, have some general timelines in mind for making career decisions. You don't need to have your future job figured out by the end of your sophomore year, but by then, you should be ready to identify a general field of study that you think you will enjoy for the rest of your undergraduate career. After your junior year, you will need to narrow the possibilities within that field, and during your senior year, you should be looking at job advertisements to determine the specific types of job that interest you.
- Don't be afraid to tell your counselor, your friends, and your family if you change your career goals. You may spend a long time, if not a lifetime, working in a profession, so you'll want to enjoy it.
- Talk to your academic counselor and your career adviser at least once each year. Not only do counselors keep students on track for graduation, but they also have good tips for thinking about career preparation.
- Take advantage of mentor programs. A mentor will give you

insights into the real world of work. Someone who is in the profession right now can tell you what skills she uses on a daily basis, how she got where she is today, and what skills she will need for the job she wants tomorrow.

- When you apply for internships, look for a position that will allow opportunities for on-the-job observation and hands-on experience.
- Talk to the professors in your major. They know the field, they know the kind of jobs their former students have taken, and they can predict how the profession is likely to change in the near future. They can also write letters of recommendation that will support your job or graduate school applications.

CHAPTER 12

"I'll *Always* Be Here If You Need Me"

Mentoring for a Lifetime

The last few months of the senior year create a whole new set of concerns for parents. Your student talks convincingly about goals and deadlines, but you see little progress. The hands-off parenting methods that were just beginning to feel comfortable now seem completely wrong. All the self-confidence you saw in your child a year ago is evaporating.

When your child was graduating from high school, you were involved in all the decisions. Now, as your student makes the transition from college to a job or graduate school, the family role is much less obvious. Students *want* advice, but they no longer feel that they should *need* their parents' advice. They have been making all kinds of decisions during the past few years, but until now, the impact has never seemed quite so significant. Faced with multiple opportunities, all of which seem to have potential both for raging success and dashing failure, they would be happy to turn the decision over to someone else. "What should I do? I can't figure it out. *You* tell me!"

At this stage of your child's life, your responsibility is primarily to maintain a respectful distance, encourage your child to think carefully about all aspects of a decision, and support the choices he or she makes. Unfortunately, when it comes to your child's career decisions, you have three strikes against you:

- You don't know all the details, so you cannot make a fully informed recommendation. If, for example, your child is weighing two job offers, the company offering a better salary might seem to you to be the better choice. However, a highly supportive supervisor could make the lower-paying job the better option in the long run.
- You are still too emotionally involved to offer an unbiased opinion. An opportunity that will bring your child closer to home may seem more appealing to you than the position halfway across the country.
- If your student heeds your advice and something goes wrong, you will feel responsible.

You can, however, ask some thoughtful questions to help your child assess her choices. If she is comparing job offers in different communities, you can suggest that she consider cost-of-living and moving expenses in addition to the salary range. Ask if she has compared benefit packages. Find out if she has decided how long she might want to stay in the position and has investigated how each position could advance her career in the next few years.

You know, even if your child does not, that the career decisions she is making today are just the beginning, and her direction can—and probably will—change in the future. She is still young. If today's choice turns out not to be the best, she can start over tomorrow with greater wisdom based on this experience.

POISED BETWEEN COLLEGE AND THE REAL WORLD

Students start college with high expectations and lofty goals. As graduating seniors, they look back on their achievements, and the reality can be a disappointment. Belinda had always said she would go to medical school, but her college grades didn't qualify her for any of the top-ranked schools she had hoped to attend. "Do I want to get a medical degree from some school no one has ever heard of? Maybe I should try something else altogether. My English grades were always good."

Occasionally, a student's carefully constructed plans are thrown off track by circumstances beyond his control. Len was graduating with a teaching certificate just when the state was spiraling into a major economic recession. Teachers were being laid off, and he couldn't even get a job interview. "Check back in August," everyone told him. "We'll know better by then whether we'll have any openings."

And sometimes, heavy competition for the best jobs requires applicants to sacrifice short-term benefits for the promise of long-term potential. Valerie's double major in organizational communications and human relations qualified her for a promising two-year training program at a Fortune 500 firm, but the company would only tell her that she would be assigned to one of three programs—in Phoenix, Minneapolis, or San Francisco. "On the salary they're offering, I could afford to live in Phoenix or Minneapolis," Valerie said. "But there's no way I could pay for an apartment in San Francisco. How do I accept the job without knowing for sure where they're sending me?"

Just when students are trying to make career or graduate school choices, they're confronting the emotions that come with leaving the first home they have created on their own. The friendships that develop in college are intense. Students feel extremely close to their roommates and their study partners, not to mention a boyfriend or girlfriend. Campus is comfortable, professors have become treasured mentors, and now they must think about leaving it all behind.

And many simply are not ready to face the responsibilities of adult life; they're still busy enjoying college. The idea of leaving school, beginning a career, and finally becoming a grown-up seems like a script for a TV sit-com. It's a nice image, but what does it have to do with reality?

Questioning Carefully

Everyone's expectations are high for the prospective graduate. Throughout the senior year, all the relatives and family friends will be asking "What are you going to do after graduation?" "Do you have a job yet?" If students don't have a job lined up, the questions begin to feel like a personal attack.

Students react more positively when the questions are less direct: "Do you think you'll stay in Boston after you graduate?" "How does the job market look for students in your major?" You will still get the update on your child's plans, but your student won't hear your questions as criticism.

POST-COLLEGE PARENTING

Some families can afford to support their children beyond graduation, but most are ready for their sons and daughters to be on their own. A few will finance their child's graduate program, while others believe that post-graduate studies are the student's responsibility. There are families who will help their child settle into a first home, but others can barely afford a graduation gift.

Your son or daughter should be well aware by now of the family financial situation. Problems usually occur only when students are unclear of expectations or when they do not know that family circumstances have changed.

Richard never considered finances to be a serious issue. His family had owned a successful printing company for three generations. Not long before Richard finished college, his parents decided to sell the business and retire. Computers had cut into the demand for printing, and as costs for new labor and new equipment kept going up, it made sense to sell out. In fact, they learned, they probably should have sold the business a few years earlier. They received much less for the sale than they had hoped.

Meanwhile, Richard had planned a post-graduation trip to Europe with friends. By August, he was having so much fun that he decided to turn in his plane ticket and extend his trip an extra couple of months. In late October, cold, rainy weather caught up with him in Amsterdam, and he called home to ask his parents to put enough money on his debit card to buy some warm clothes and pay for a flight home.

He did not expect his mother's explosive reaction. "We haven't heard from you in a month, and now you're calling to ask for money? I'll give you enough for a ticket to come home, but that's it. We're on a retirement income, and we just don't have extra money. You're twenty-two now, and it's time you were responsible for yourself."

Graduating seniors probably have a sense of what their own debts will be after college, but they may not understand how much their parents are still paying. They are unlikely to know what your financial obligations are to your other children. They are consumed by the responsibility of their debts and commitments, and it's hard for them to think beyond their own financial situation.

Sometime during the senior year, or at least soon after graduation, a frank discussion about debts, payment plans, and when or how you can help will clarify the issues for everyone concerned:

- When do you expect your student to assume all his or her financial responsibilities?
- How will college loans be handled?
- What happens if there's an emergency?
- Under what conditions will you help your child financially in the future?

There will be times when unusual circumstances or your child's own choices put you in the position of deciding whether or not to intervene. A year after she graduated from college, Cathy was working as a reporter at a small daily paper. She signed a lease on a one-bedroom garden apartment in a nice housing complex, and she traded in the seven-year-old station wagon her parents had handed down to her for the red sports coupe she had always wanted.

When her coworkers asked her to go out for lunch, though, she never ordered anything but a glass of ice water and a cup of soup. "And can I get extra crackers, please?" she would ask.

With her monthly rent, car payment, and college loan payment, Cathy's salary left her with almost no spending money. She had been a "poor college student" for four years, so she was used to stretching every dollar, but she was not prepared for this kind of budget constraint. Most frustrating, her credit card debt was mounting, and there was no end in sight.

Parents can find this time of their child's life more difficult than the college years. "Should we help her out?" Cathy's mother asked her husband. "Maybe we could take over her school loans for a year. I hate to see her struggle like this."

"We can't be there to bail her out for the rest of her life," he answered. "We have two other kids to put through college. Cathy could have found a cheaper apartment, and she certainly didn't need to buy that new car as soon as she graduated. She's got to learn to handle her money."

You might reach a point when you have to ask the inevitable question: Should your child move back home? You know it's always there as the backup plan. Some students even think that moving home is a terrific idea. All the pressure would be off. If there's no rent to pay and no groceries to buy, any job should provide enough to live on. As college loans come due, it's much easier to chip away at the debts when there are no monthly housing payments or utility bills. For most students, though, going home is the last resort and only a temporary solution. Today's college graduates saw their older cousins, siblings, or neighbors—members of the Slacker Generation—move back home after college or when jobs fell through, and it looked like failure. If students decide to move back, they usually say they will stay only until their credit card debts are paid off or until they have enough money saved to make a start somewhere else.

The pangs of parenting will continue, no matter how old your child is. If he takes a new job in a city where he doesn't know anyone, you will worry that he is all alone with no one to help in an emergency. When she moves into a new apartment or buys a house, you will feel a strong urge to visit, or at least see pictures. You will need a visual image of your child in any new setting before you can feel entirely comfortable. When something bad happens to your son or daughter—job loss, illness, the breakup of a relationship—you will, indeed, feel the pain. You will also share the joy and pride of all the successes—a promising relationship, a new job, wedding plans, or the birth of a child.

If you find yourself wondering if you're saying and doing the right things for your adult child, be assured that your doubts are entirely normal and that all parents make their children crazy on occasion. The mother of one doctoral candidate noted, "It's *still* hard to figure out when my daughter is telling me something because she wants my advice, and when she just wants me to listen while she thinks out loud. I will *always* mess that up!"

You are not the only mentor your child will have during his life—by the time he leaves college, he will know that he can turn to his favorite professor, a former supervisor, and his college friends for advice and support. College alumni chapters or fraternity and sorority national organizations encourage former students to seek out support from other alumni throughout the country.

Nevertheless, your child appreciates you, possibly more than you know. After all those years of trying to break away from family ties and become independent, college graduates come to the realization that they still want their parents' love and support.

At a graduation reception for student leaders, two seniors were talking about their post-college plans. Mike was telling his friend that he had decided to stay in Minneapolis for law school. "I know I'm going to want to work in Minnesota after I get my law degree, so it's only logical to go to school here and take the bar exam here."

"Do you really want to stay in Minnesota for the rest of your life?" his friend asked. "Don't you want to get away from this cold weather?"

"Someplace warm would be nice, but my family is here," Mike said. "I'll admit, sometimes I curse my ancestors for settling in such a cold place, but I know I want to live near my family. Can't help it. I love 'em."

"Yeah, I know what you mean," said the other student, looking at the floor and shuffling awkwardly. "I love my parents, too. It took a while to realize it, but they're about the best people I know."

QUICK TIPS FOR STUDENTS

- For the entire last half of your senior year, people will ask repeatedly, "What will you do after graduation?" Don't take it

personally. You can use their question as a networking opportunity: "I'm looking for a job. Do you happen to know anyone
in my field I can talk to?"

- Do not panic if you don't have a job lined up before graduation. The summer after graduation is a good time to fine-tune
the résumé, carefully search job listings, and make sure you
have good recommendations from professors or former
employers. A lot of jobs open up during the summer. Use the
months after graduation for the job hunt, not for berating
yourself!

- Do not feel bad about taking a "flexible" job after graduation.
You need a job that will allow time off for interviews when
they come up.

- Talk with your family about post-college finances so that
you're clear on their expectations.

- Tell your parents you appreciate them. They need to hear
things like that sometimes.

The Four-Year College Calendar

Each of the college years presents new issues as students develop academic and life skills. Parents will not always know precisely what problems their child is facing at any given time, but there are some common issues that most students face during the four years of their academic career.

FRESHMAN ISSUES

The freshman year is all about change and self-discovery. The critical issues for freshmen involve time management, setting limits, and study skills.

Time Management

First-year students often struggle to balance studying, socializing, and personal time. All are important.

Ultimately, the goal is to master the academic responsibilities, but it is important to make time for friendships. Students *do* learn more from other people than from classroom lectures, and college provides an amazing opportunity to meet other young adults and to learn about their backgrounds and dreams. Students also need time just for themselves. Some personal time to exercise, listen to music, or read a book just for fun allows students to find the energy to handle everything else in their schedules. The occasional quiet hour also gives them a chance to figure out how everything they're learning fits with their own value system and personality.

Setting Limits

When a little of something brings pleasure, it's hard to know when to stop. During the first weeks of college, students are tempted to stay up too late or sleep too much, eat too much or skip meals entirely, socialize excessively or even study too hard. Balance is critical.

Study Skills

The read-and-review or memorization methods that worked in high school are not enough to succeed in college. College classes require that students know how to analyze and think critically about what they read. It's not enough to read and understand the day's assignment from the American history textbook; students must be able to explain how the material relates to this morning's news headlines and what it might mean about the human condition. Study skills workshops are available at most colleges, and they are not just for borderline students. Students who are open to finding new ways to study and learn will reap the rewards.

SOPHOMORE ISSUES

During the second year, students are more comfortable. They question themselves less about daily concerns. Nevertheless, students feel that they should have everything under control, but they know they don't. All the excitement and challenge of the first year is gone, and the adrenaline rush of transition is gone.

The traditional sophomore slump hits mid-year and lingers through the spring.

The critical issues for sophomores involve academic complacency, personal and financial risk, and changing interests and goals.

Academic Complacency

During their first year, students learned that they could get by with B's and C's. As sophomores, they are comfortable with average work. Sophomores are usually continuing to fulfill their general academic requirements, and they feel as if they are biding their time until they get into their major. The grades they earn this year, however, can make all the difference when they declare a major or apply for graduate school. Some selective upper division (junior- and senior-level) programs require a minimum grade point average during the first two years. Graduate programs almost always look at overall accomplishments. Some slack may be allowed for freshman year adjustment, but students who are lax the second year can lose future opportunities.

Personal and Financial Risk

Sophomores often take risks that they didn't dare to attempt as freshmen and that they won't feel the need to take as juniors. This is a year when financial problems can become compounded, and when relationships get out of control. They may have signed up for three credit cards as freshmen, but this year they start using them.

Changing Interests and Goals

All the introductory courses students take during their first two years of college have a purpose. In addition to giving them a strong academic foundation, the courses provide a glimpse of the many different aspects within a single broad subject. Sophomores are ripe for identifying their passion in life, and they still have the time to change their minds.

JUNIOR ISSUES

The junior year can be the best. In ideal circumstances, students are in their major, taking classes that interest them. They know the campus, they have learned the routine, and they feel as though life is under control. Juniors are taking leadership positions in campus organizations, and they have friends everywhere they look. Parents seem to worry least about juniors. They can see that their children are making progress. Their students have formally declared a field of study and seem to have a plan for at least the next two years. Like their students, parents have adjusted to the college processes. They know the financial routines, and they trust their student's ability to handle any problems that crop up.

The critical issues for juniors involve disillusionment, regrets, and intimate relationships.

Disillusionment

Students who have been waiting to take classes in their major might be disappointed to find that some of the courses they've been looking forward to are not as exciting as they expected. It can be frustrating for students to acknowledge that they are still learning theory, not applying skills.

Regrets

As juniors, students come to recognize the consequences of their earlier failures. The D in calculus that felt like a victory two years ago—"At least I passed, and I don't ever have to take another math class!"—now looks like an eternal albatross. Students try to figure out how they can possibly raise their grades up to 3.5, and they realize they don't have enough classes left to improve that much. When they look at the three classes they dropped during their first two years in school, they see that they won't be able to graduate on schedule. There is no way to make up 12 credit hours without committing to another semester on campus. This is the year when students also begin to figure out how much debt they will have when they graduate from college. Until now, it was only a number. Now, as they consider the monthly cost of an apartment and the price of a new car, they see what their college debt will mean to their post-graduate lifestyle.

Intimate Relationships

During childhood, children turned to parents for support and guidance. Throughout the teen years, they relied increasingly on their friends. Now as they consider the future, they begin to realize that they will leave family and college friends behind when they move into a career or go on to graduate school. Intimate relationships feel like a lifeline from the present into the unknown future. Although they know rationally that they have plenty of time to find a life partner, it is still common for students during their junior year to make commitments for the future or to feel devastated when a relationship ends.

SENIOR ISSUES

Seniors know their niche in the school, and perhaps they have made their mark by leading an organization or earning honors for the college. Just when things should be comfortable, though, they are sweating the next steps. Deadlines come quickly for graduate school exams and applications, and the weight of finding a job hangs over their heads.

The critical issues for seniors involve balancing priorities, racing against time, and facing the unknown.

Balancing Priorities

Students who neglected to take all the required lower-division courses must complete them before they can graduate. They are annoyed to be spending time on sophomore-level classes, but they must fulfill the requirements. Meanwhile, they have senior papers or major research projects due. Every new assignment seems to get in the way of a previous commitment.

Racing Against Time

The college career that once seemed to stretch way into the future is now boiled down to eight short months. When fall semester begins, seniors already feel as if they're behind schedule. If they're planning to attend graduate school, they should already have narrowed down their selections. In short order, they must take Graduate Record Exams or professional school tests, and it takes time to write a compelling grad school application. Students who will be looking for a job need to begin writing a résumé and researching possible openings. Whether they will go to grad school or into a career, everyone needs to find professors who will write letters of recommendation.

Facing the Unknown

With the end of school in sight, students begin to fear the future. If they will be moving to another area, they will be leaving everything that is familiar. They are not just finding a new job or enrolling in a new school, they will also be looking for a new apartment, meeting new people, starting new routines. They will be expected to make payments on educational loans. Even if they are staying in the same town, life will change. Friends will be leaving. They will not be part of the same community. It's time to accept responsibility.

For More Information

BOOKS

Ahmad, Shaheena. 1997. *The Yale Daily News Guide to Succeeding in College.* New York: Simon & Schuster.

Bragdon, Allen D., and David Gamon. 1999. *How Sharp Is Your Pencil?* Bass River, Mass.: Brainwaves Books.

Coburn, Karen Levin, and Madge Lawrence Treeter. 1997. *Letting Go: A Parents' Guide to Understanding the College Years.* New York: HarperPerennial.

Combs, Patrick, and Jack Canfield. 2000. *Major in Success: Make College Easier, Fire Up Your Dreams, and Get a Very Cool Job.* Berkeley, Calif.: Ten Speed Press.

Dobkin, Rachel, and Shana Sippy. 1995. *The College Woman's Handbook: Educating Ourselves.* New York: Workman.

Griffin, Carolyn Welch; Marian J. Wirth; and Arthur G. Wirth. 1997. *Beyond Acceptance: Parents of Lesbians and Gays Talk about Their Experience.* New York: St. Martin's Press.

Harris, Marcia B., and Sharon Jones. 1996. *The Parent's Crash Course in Career Planning.* Lincolnwood, Ill: VGM Career Horizons.

Howe, Neil, and William Straus. 2000. *Millennials Rising: The Next Great Generation.* New York: Vintage Books.

Jamison, Kay Redfield. 1999. *Night Falls Fast: Understanding Suicide.* New York: Vintage Books.

Jennings, Kevin, with Pat Shapiro, M.S.W. 2003. *Always My Child: A Parent's*

Guide to Understanding Your Gay, Lesbian, Bisexual, Transgendered, or Questioning Son or Daughter. New York: Simon & Schuster.

Kobliner, Beth. 1996. Get a Financial Life: Personal Finance in Your Twenties and Thirties. New York: Simon & Schuster, Fireside.

Light, Richard. 2001. Making the Most of College: Students Speak Out. Cambridge, Mass.: Harvard University Press.

Litt, Ann Selkowitz. 2000. The College Student's Guide to Eating Well on Campus. Bethesda, Md.: Tulip Hill Press.

McDougall, Bryce. 1998. My Child Is Gay: How Parents React When They Hear the News. New York: Unwin Hyman.

Nuwer, Hank. 1999. Wrongs of Passage: Fraternities, Sororities, Hazing, and Binge Drinking. Bloomington, Ind.: Indiana University Press.

Peterson's Study Abroad. 2002. Lawrenceville, N.J.: Peterson's Guides.

Quinn, Patricia O. 2001. ADD and the College Student: A Guide for High School and College Students with Attention Deficit Disorder. Washington, D.C.: Magination Press.

Rickgarn, Ralph L.V. 1994. Perspectives on College Student Suicide. Amityville, N.Y.: Baywood.

Scheele, Adele M. 2000. Jumpstart Your Career in College: Build the Skills to Build Your Future. New York: Kaplan.

Schneider, Barbara, and David Stevenson. 1999. The Ambitious Generation: America's Teenagers, Motivated but Directionless. New Haven, Conn.: Yale University Press.

WEB SITES

Alcohol Issues
   www.collegedrinkingprevention.gov
   www.edc.org/hec
   www.factsontap.org
Campus Safety
   www.CampusSafety.org/
   www.ncvc.org/
   www.ncvc.org/src/index.html
   www.usfa.fema.gov/dhtml/public/campus.cfm

College Parenting
   www.collegeparents.org
Eating Disorders
   www.something-fishy.org
Finances
   www.savingforcollege.com
Gay, Lesbian, Bisexual, Transgender Issues
   www.pflag.org
Hazing
   www.stophazing.org
National Student Exchange
   www.nse.org
Service Learning and Community Service
   www.servicelearning.org
Sex
   www.goaskalice.columbia.edu
Sexual Assault
   www.rainn.org
Study Abroad
   www.cdc.gov
   www.travel.state.gov

Notes

1. Adapted from "How to Spot a Loser Lover," the Aurora Center, and "Is It an Invitation, or Is It Coercion?" Interfaith Campus Coalition, University of Minnesota.

2. National Center for Public Policy and Higher Education, *Measuring Up 2000: The State-by-State Report Card for Higher Education*, available at http://measuringup2000.highereducation.org/completion.cfm.

3. Michael Pare, "Making College Achievable for All Is Their Goal," *Providence Business News*, November 6, 2000, p. 4.

4. A student is considered dependent unless he or she is twenty-four years old, married, a graduate student, a veteran, an orphan, or a ward of the court, or has legal dependents.

5. Calculated at www.bankrate.com

6. Eric Hoover, "The Lure of Easy Credit Leaves More Students Struggling with Debt," *Chronicle of Higher Education* 47 (40), June 15, 2001, p. A35.

7. Ibid.

8. Credit Sense: Responsible Selling and Use of Personal Debt Project, 2002, St. Paul, Minnesota.

9. National Institute on Drug Abuse, survey conducted by the University of Michigan, 2001, available at www.drugabuse.gov/Infofax/HSYouth trends.html. Accessed April 23, 2002.

10. Diana Jean Schemo, "Study Calculates the Effects of College Drinking in U.S.," *The New York Times*, April 10, 2002, p. A16.

11. National Institute on Alcohol Abuse and Alcoholism, 2002, "A Call to Action: Changing the Culture of Drinking at U.S. Colleges," available at www.collegedrinkingprevention.gov.

12. Henry Wechsler et al., "College Binge Drinking in the 1990s: A Continuing Problem—Results of the Harvard School of Public Health 1999 College Alcohol Study," *Journal of American College Health* 48(5), 2000, pp. 199–210.

13. Kenneth J. Sher, Bruce D. Bartholow, and Shivani Nanda, "Short- and Long-Term Effects of Fraternity and Sorority Membership: A Social Norms Perspective," *Psychology of Addictive Behaviors* 15(1), March 2001, pp. 42–51.

14. National Institute on Alcohol Abuse and Alcoholism, www.college drinkingprevention.gov.

15. Aaron P. Turner, Mary E. Larimer, and Irwin G. Sarason, "Family Risk Factors for Alcohol-Related Consequences and Poor Adjustment in Fraternity and Sorority Members: Explore the Role of Parent-Child Conflict," *Journal of Studies on Alcohol* 61, November 2000, p. 818.

16. Bonnie S. Fisher, Francis T. Cullen, and Michael G. Turner, *The Sexual Victimization of College Women*, U.S. Department of Justice, December 2000.

17. Alex P. Kellogg, "'Safe Sex Fatigue' Grows Among Gay Students," *Chronicle of Higher Education*, January 18, 2002, p. A37.

18. "Encouraging College Students to Exercise," *USA Today Magazine*, September 2001, p. 9.

19. Centers for Disease Control and Prevention, "Meningococcal Disease Among College Students," October 1999.

20. "Meningococcal Infection in College Students," *Internal Medicine Alert* 23(18), September 29, 2001, p. 140.

21. Lise M. Stevens, "Adolescent Suicide," *Journal of the American Medical Association* 286(24), December 26, 2001, p. 3194.

22. Robert Aseltine et al., "Life After High School: Development, Stress, and Well-Being," in Gotlib and Wheaton, *Stress and Adversity over the Life Course* (Cambridge: Cambridge University Press, 1997), pp. 197–214.

23. "Fast Track," *American Demographics*, April 1, 2001, p. 24.

Bibliography

BOOKS AND PUBLICATIONS

American Demographics. 2001. "Fast Track." April 1, p. 24.

American Medical Association. 2001. *Partner or Foe? The Alcohol Industry, Youth Alcohol Problems, and Alcohol Policy Strategies.* Policy briefing paper.

Aseltine, Robert; Susan Gore; Mary Ellen Colton; B. Lin. 1997. "Life After High School: Development, Stress, and Well-Being." In Gotlib and Wheaton, *Stress and Adversity over the Life Course.* Cambridge: Cambridge University Press, pp. 197–214.

Astin, Alexander W., and G. Erlandson. 1993. *Four Critical Years Revisited.* San Francisco: Jossey-Bass.

Burtley, Cleo. 2000. "Benefit Helps Parents with College Process." *Business Insurance.* September 18, p. 3.

Business Week. 2000. "Working Toward a Major in Debt." September 25, p. 192 E10.

Carter, Gertrude, and Jeffrey Winseman. 2001. "A Prescription for Healing the Whole Student." *Chronicle of Higher Education* 47(47), August 3, p. B24.

Chickering, Arthur W., and Linda Reisser. 1993. *Education and Identity.* San Francisco: Jossey-Bass.

Crary, David. "Police Take Cyberstalking More Seriously." *Nando Times.* http://www.nandotimes.com/nation/v-text/story/36183p-589960c.html (accessed July 2, 2001).

Credit Sense: Responsible Selling and Use of Personal Debt Project. Sponsored by the Saint Paul Foundation, St. Paul, Minnesota. Data for the project were collected from 2001 to 2002. A report of the project's findings is due to be published in 2003.

Daniel, Bonnie, and B. Ross Scott, editors. 2001. *Consumers, Adversaries, and Partners: Working with the Families of Undergraduates.* San Francisco: Jossey-Bass.

Davis, Barbara D. 1999. "Encouraging Commuter Student Connectivity." *Business Communication Quarterly* 62(2) June, pp. 74–78.

Dobkin, Rachel, and Shana Sippy. 1995. *The College Woman's Handbook: Educating Ourselves.* New York: Workman.

Evans, Nancy J.; Deanna S. Forney; and Florence Guido-Dibrito. 1998. *Student Development in College: Theory, Research, and Practice.* San Francisco: Jossey-Bass.

Fahey, Marge. 2001. "Checks and Balances." *Insight on the News* 17(21), June 4, p. 31.

Fisher, Bonnie S.; Francis T. Cullen; and Michael G. Turner. 2000. *The Sexual Victimization of College Women.* U.S. Department of Justice.

Futurist, The. 2001. "The Web-Connected Generation." September, p. 9.

Gerdes, Eugenia. 2001. "Managing Time in a Liberal Education." *Liberal Education* 87(2), Spring, pp. 52–57.

Gordon, Virginia N. 1984. *The Undecided College Student: An Academic and Career Advising Challenge.* Springfield, Ill.: Charles C. Thomas.

Hoover, Eric. 2001. "The Lure of Easy Credit Leaves More Students Struggling with Debt." *Chronicle of Higher Education* 47(40), June 15, pp. A35–36.

Howe, Neil, and William Straus. 2000. *Millennials Rising: The Next Great Generation.* New York: Vintage Books.

Internal Medicine Alert. 2001. "Meningococcal Infection in College Students." September 29, p. 140.

Jamison, Kay Redfield. 1999. *Night Falls Fast: Understanding Suicide.* New York: Vintage Books.

Kellogg, Alex P. 2002. "'Safe Sex Fatigue' Grows among Gay Students." *Chronicle of Higher Education,* January 18, pp. A37–38.

Kissee, James E.; Stanley D. Murphy; Gloria L. Bonner; and Laura C. Murley. 2000. "Effects of Family Origin Dynamics on College Freshmen." *College Student Journal* 34(2), June, p. 172.

Kobliner, Beth. 1996. *Get a Financial Life: Personal Finance in Your Twenties and Thirties.* New York: Simon & Schuster, Fireside.

Kuh, George D. 1994. *Student Learning Outside the Classroom: Transcending Artificial Boundaries.* ASHE-ERIC Higher Education Report No. 8. Washington, D.C.: U.S. Department of Education, Office of Educational Research and Improvement.

Leibman-Smith, Joan. 2001. "Is It September Yet? Even the Best Kids Can Get Ugly As Senior Year Ends." *Newsweek,* May 14, p. 61.

Light, Richard. 2001. *Making the Most of College: Students Speak Out.* Cambridge, Mass.: Harvard University Press.

Luzzo, Darrell Anthony. 2000. *Career Counseling of College Students: An Empirical Guide to Strategies That Work.* Washington, D.C.: American Psychological Association.

Maslow, Abraham. 1971. *The Farther Reaches of Human Nature.* New York: Viking.

National Center for Public Policy and Higher Education. 2000. *Measuring Up 2000: The State-by-State Report Card for Higher Education.* Available at http://measuringup2000.highereducation.org/completion.cfm (accessed March 3, 2002).

National Institute on Alcohol Abuse and Alcoholism. 2002. "A Call to Action: Changing the Culture of Drinking at U.S. Colleges." Available at http://www.collegedrinkingprevention.gov (accessed April 23, 2002).

National Institute on Drug Abuse, 2001. "High School and Youth Trends: 2001 Monitoring the Future Study." Available at http://www.drugabuse.gov/Infofax?HYYouthtrends.html (accessed April 23, 2002).

Nelson, Wendy L.; Honore M. Hughes; Barry Katz; and H. Russell Searight. 1999. "Anorexic Eating Attitudes and Behaviors of Male and Female College Students." *Adolescence* 34(35), Fall, p. 621.

Newton, Fred B. 2000. "The New Student." *About Campus* 5(5), November–December, pp. 8–15.

Pare, Michael. 2000. "Making College Achievable for All Is Their Goal." *Providence Business News* 15(29), November 6, p. 4.

Pascarella, Ernest T., and Patrick T. Terenzini. 1991. *How College Affects Students: Findings and Insights from Twenty Years of Research.* San Francisco: Jossey-Bass.

Randinelli, Tracey. 2002. "Making the Grade: Ace Your College Classes with This Advice on Choosing Courses, Selecting a Major, Writing Papers, and Dealing with Professors." *Careers and Colleges* 22(4), March, pp. 32–37.

Rickgarn, Ralph L.V. 1994. *Perspectives on College Student Suicide.* Amityville, N.Y.: Baywood.

———. 2001. "The Issue Is Suicide." The Suicide Awareness Fund, University of Minnesota.

Schemo, Diana Jean. 2002. "Study Calculates the Effects of College Drinking in U.S.," *The New York Times,* April 10, p. A16.

Schneider, Barbara, and David Stevenson. 1999. *The Ambitious Generation: America's Teenagers, Motivated but Directionless.* New Haven, Conn.: Yale University Press.

Sher, Kenneth J.; Bruce D. Bartholow; and Shivani Nanda. 2001. "Short- and Long-Term Effects of Fraternity and Sorority Membership: A Social Norms Perspective." *Psychology of Addictive Behaviors* 15(1), March, pp. 42–51.

Smith, Lynn. 2001. "Finding Good in 'Normal.'" *Los Angeles Times,* June 12, p. 1.

Stepp, Laura Sessions. 2002. "Perfect Problems." *Washington Post.* May 5, p. F1.

Stevens, Lise M. 2001. "Adolescent Suicide." *Journal of the American Medical Association* 286(24), December 26, p. 3194.

Tederman, James S. 1997. *Advice from the Dean: A Personal Perspective on the Philosophy, Roles, and Approaches of a Dean at a Small, Private, Liberal Arts College.* Washington, D.C.: National Association of Student Personnel Administrators.

Tinto, Vincent. 1993. *Leaving College: Rethinking the Causes and Cures of Student Attrition.* Chicago: University of Chicago Press.

Tobin, Eugene M. 2001. "Don't Ban Fraternities, Embrace Them. Embrace Them Closely." *Chronicle of Higher Education* 48(16), December 14, p. B24.

Turner, Aaron P.; Mary E. Larimer; and Irwin G. Sarason. 2000. "Family Risk Factors for Alcohol-Related Consequences and Poor Adjustment in Fraternity and Sorority Members: Explore the Role of Parent-Child Conflict." *Journal of Studies on Alcohol* 61(6), November, p. 818.

Turrentine, Cathryn Coree; Stacey L. Schnure.; D. David Ostroth; Jeanine A. Ward-Roof. 2000. "The Parent Project: What Parents Want from the College Experience." *NASPA Journal* 38(1), Fall, pp. 31–43.

Turrisi, Rob; Kimberly A. Wiersma; and Kelli K. Hughes. 2000. "Binge-Drinking-Related Consequences in College Students: Role of Drinking Beliefs and Mother-Teen Communications." *Psychology of Addictive Behaviors* 14(4), December, pp. 342–355.

University of Michigan. 2001. *National Institute on Drug Abuse Survey, 2001*. Available at http://www.drugabuse.gov/Infofax/HSYouthtrends.html (accessed April 23 2002).

USA Today Magazine. 2001. "Encouraging College Students to Exercise." September, p. 9.

U.S. Government Accounting Office. 2001. *Consumer Finance: College Students and Credit Cards*. June, GAO-01-773.

Wechsler, Henry, et al. 2000. "College Binge Drinking in the 1990s: A Continuing Problem—Results of the Harvard School of Public Health 1999 College Alcohol Study." *Journal of American College Health* 48(5), pp. 199–210.

Weiss, Larry J. 1989. *Parents Programs: How to Create Lasting Ties*. Washington, D.C.: Council for Advancement and Support of Higher Education.

Wildavsky, Ben. 1999. "Is That the Real Price?" *U.S. News & World Report*. September 6, p. 64.

Wood, Phillip K., et al. 1997. "Predicting Academic Problems in College from Freshman Alcohol Involvement." *Journal of Studies on Alcohol* 58(2), March, pp. 200–210.

INDEX

About the Author

Marjorie Savage is director of the Parent Program at the University of Minnesota—a pioneering liaison program that reaches out to parents of the school's 28,000 undergraduates (www.parent.umn.edu). She lives in Inver Grove Heights, Minnesota, where she conquered the challenges of distance-parenting her own two sons, now in their mid-twenties.